# Writing Well and
# for Your PhD a

C000133815

Prioritizing wellbeing alongside academic development, this book provides practical advice to help students write well, and be well, during their PhD and throughout their career.

In this unique book, Katherine Firth offers expert guidance on developing a writing practice and avoiding burnout, providing strategies and insights for developing a sustainable writing career beyond the PhD thesis. The book covers every stage of the academic writing process, from planning and researching, through getting words on the page, to the often unexpectedly time-consuming editing and polishing. Readers are reminded that writing a thesis is hard work, but it needn't be damaging work. Each chapter includes a toolbox of strategies and techniques, such as meditations, writing exercises and tips to maintain physical wellbeing, that will help doctoral candidates start writing and keep writing, without sacrificing their health, wellbeing or relationships.

Relevant at any stage of the writing process, this book will help doctoral students and early career researchers to produce great words that people want to read, examiners want to pass and editors want to publish.

**Katherine Firth** has been developing research writers for more than 15 years and is currently Head of Lisa Bellear House, the University of Melbourne. A co-founder of the award-winning Thesis Bootcamp program, she maintains a writing blog, *Research Degree Insiders*. She is co-author of the books *How to Fix Your Academic Writing Trouble* (2018), *Your PhD Survival Guide* (2020) and *Level Up Your Essays* (2021).

# Wellbeing and Self-care in Higher Education

Editor: **Narelle Lemon**

For more information about this series, please visit: www.routledge.com/Wellbeing-and-Self-care-in-Higher-Education/book-series/WSCHE

# Writing Well and Being Well for Your PhD and Beyond

## How to Cultivate a Strong and Sustainable Writing Practice for Life

Katherine Firth

Routledge
Taylor & Francis Group

LONDON AND NEW YORK

Designed cover image: © Getty Images

First published 2024
by Routledge
4 Park Square, Milton Park, Abingdon, Oxon OX14 4RN

and by Routledge
605 Third Avenue, New York, NY 10158

*Routledge is an imprint of the Taylor & Francis Group, an informa business*

*British Library Cataloguing-in-Publication Data*
A catalogue record for this book is available from the British Library

*Library of Congress Cataloging-in-Publication Data*
Names: Firth, Katherine, 1979- author.
Title: Writing well and being well for your PhD and beyond : how to cultivate a strong and sustainable writing practice for life / Katherine Firth.
Description: Abingdon, Oxon ; New York, NY : Routledge, 2024. | Series: Wellbeing and self-care in higher education | Includes bibliographical references and index. |
Identifiers: LCCN 2023013663 (print) | LCCN 2023013664 (ebook) | ISBN 9781032310824 (hardback) | ISBN 9781032310817 (paperback) | ISBN 9781003307945 (ebook)
Subjects: LCSH: Academic writing. | Doctoral students. | Dissertations, Academic.
Classification: LCC LB2369 .F52 2021 (print) | LCC LB2369 (ebook) | DDC 808.02--dc23/eng/20230517
LC record available at https://lccn.loc.gov/2023013663
LC ebook record available at https://lccn.loc.gov/2023013664

ISBN: 978-1-032-31082-4 (hbk)
ISBN: 978-1-032-31081-7 (pbk)
ISBN: 978-1-003-30794-5 (ebk)

DOI: 10.4324/9781003307945

Typeset in Optima
by SPi Technologies India Pvt Ltd (Straive)

This book is dedicated to the writer in your life, the writer who is you. Thank you for taking time and energy to write well and be well.

# Contents

Contents

# Illustrations

## Figures

## Tables

# Series preface

As academics, scholars, staff and colleagues working in the context of universities in the contemporary climate we are often challenged with where we place our own wellbeing. It is not uncommon to hear about burnout, stress, anxiety, pressures with workload, having too many balls in the air, toxic cultures, increasing demands, isolation, and feeling distressed (Berg and Seeber 2016; Lemon and McDonough 2018; Mountz et al. 2015). The reality is that universities are stressful places (Beer et al. 2015; Cranton and Taylor 2012; Kasworm and Bowles 2012; Mountz et al. 2015; Ryan 2013; Sullivan and Weissner 2010; Wang and Cranton 2012). McNaughton and Billot (2016) argue that the "deeply personal effects of changing roles, expectations and demands" (p. 646) have been downplayed and that academics and staff engage in constant reconstruction of their identities and work practices. It is important to acknowledge this, as much as it is to acknowledge the need to place wellbeing and self-care at the forefront of these lived experiences and situations.

Wellbeing can be approached at multiple levels including micro and macro. In placing wellbeing at the heart of the higher education workplace, self-care becomes an imperative both individually and systemically (Berg and Seeber 2016; Lemon and McDonough 2018). Self-care is most commonly oriented towards individual action to monitor and ensure personal wellbeing, however it is also a collective act. There is a plethora of different terms that are in action to describe how one approaches their wellbeing holistically (Godfrey et al. 2011). With different terminology comes different ways self-care is understood. For this collection, self-care is understood as "the actions that individuals take for themselves, on behalf of and with others in order to develop, protect, maintain and improve their health, wellbeing or wellness" (Self Care Forum 2019, para. 1). It covers a spectrum of health-related (emotional, physical, and/or spiritual) actions, including prevention, promotion and treatment, while aiming to encourage individuals to take personal responsibility for their health and to advocate for themselves and others in accessing resources and care (Knapik and Laverty 2018). Self-love, -compassion, -awareness and -regulation are significant elements of self-care. But what does this look like for those working in higher education? In this book series authors respond to the questions: *What do you do for self-care? How do you position wellbeing as part of your role in academia?*

In thinking about these questions' authors are invited to critically discuss and respond to inspiration sparked by one or more of the following questions:

- How do we bring self-regulation to how we approach our work?
- How do we create a compassionate workplace in academia?
- What does it mean for our work when we are aware and enact self-compassion?
- What awareness has occurred that has disrupted the way we approach work?
- Where do mindful intentions sit?
- How do we shift the rhetoric of "this is how it has always been" in relation to over working, and indiscretions between workload and approaches to workload?
- How do we counteract the traditional narrative of over work?
- How do we create and sustain a healthier approach?
- How can we empower the "I" and "we" as we navigate self-care as a part of who we are as academics?
- How can we promote a curiosity about how we approach self-care?
- What changes do we need to make?
- How can we approach self-care with energy and promote shifts in how we work individually, collectively and systemically?

The purpose of this book series is to:

- Place academic wellbeing and self-care at the heart of discussions around working in higher education.
- Provide a diverse range of strategies for how to put in place wellbeing and self-care approaches as an academic.

- Provide a narrative connection point for readers from a variety of back-grounds in academia.
- Highlight lived experiences and honour the voice of those working in higher education.
- Provide a visual narrative that supports connection to authors' lived experience(s).
- Contribute to the conversation on ways that wellbeing and self-care can be positioned in the work that those working in higher education do.
- Highlight new ways of working in higher education that disrupt current tensions that neglect wellbeing.

# References

LE Beer, K Rodriguez, C Taylor, N Martinez-Jones, J Griffin, TR Smith, M Lamar and R Anaya, 'Awareness, Integration and Interconnectedness', *Journal of Transformative Education*, 13:2, 161–185. 2015.

M Berg and BK Seeber, *The Slow Professor: Challenging the Culture of Speed in the Academy*. University of Toronto Press, 2016.

P Cranton and EW Taylor, 'Transformative Learning Theory: Seeking a more Unified Theory', in EW Taylor and P Cranton, editor, *The Handbook of Transformative Learning*, pp. 3–20. Jossey-Bass, 2012.

CM Godfrey, MB Harrison, R Lysaght, M Lamb, ID Graham and P Oakley, 'The Experience of Self-Care: A Systematic Review', *JBI Library of Systematic Reviews* 8:34, 1351–1460. 2011. http://www.ncbi.nlm.nih.gov/pubmed/27819888

N Lemon and S McDonough, editors, *Mindfulness in the Academy: Practices and Perspectives from Scholars*. Springer, 2018.

C Kasworm and T Bowles, 'Fostering Transformative Learning in Higher Education Settings', In E Taylor and P Cranton, editors, *The Handbook of Transformative Learning*, pp. 388–407. Sage, 2012.

K Knapik and A Laverty, 'Self-Care Individual, Relational, and Political Sensibilities', in MA Henning, CU Krägeloh, R Dryer, F Moir, DR Billington and AG Hill, editors. *Wellbeing in Higher Education: Cultivating a Healthy Lifestyle Among Faculty and Students*. Routledge, 2018.

S M McNaughton and J Billot, 'Negotiating Academic Teacher Identity Shifts During Higher Education Contextual Change', *Teaching in Higher Education* 21:6, 644–658. 2016.

A Mountz, A Bonds, B Mansfield, J Loyd, J Hyndman and M Watton-Roberts, 'For Slow Scholarship: A Feminist Politics of Resistance Through Collective Action in the Neoliberal University', *ACME: An International E-Journal of Critical Geographies* 14:4, 1235–1259. 2015.

M Ryan, 'The Pedagogical Balancing Act: Teaching Reflection in Higher Education', *Teaching in Higher Education* 18, 144–155. 2013.

Self Care Forum. Self Care Forum: Home. 2019. http://www.selfcareforum.org/

LG Sullivan and CA Weissner, 'Learning To Be Reflective Leaders: A Case Study from the NCCHC Hispanic Leadership Fellows Program', in DL Wallin, editor, Special issue: *Leadership in an Era of Change. New Directions for Community Colleges*, No. 149, pp. 41–50. Jossey-Bass, 2010.

VC Wang and P Cranton, 'Promoting and Implementing Self-Directed Learning (SDL): An Effective Adult Education Model', *International Journal of Adult Vocational Education and Technology* 3, 16–25. 2012.

# A note from the series editor

There is an awareness that comes with writing well and being well. This awareness has us cultivating a consciousness that situates both the acts of *writing well* and *being well* together. It sounds obvious but, for many of us, it is not. Too often we forget, skip (intentionally or by mistake), rush, not value or even not know that we needed to value our wellbeing. Phew, I'm exhausted! Exhausted in a good way, as this is appreciating the complexity that comes when we are mindfully present in our approach to writing while holistically valuing our heart, mind, body, and spirit. With this awareness comes an enabling that supports the creation of new words on a page and a cultivation of renewed ways of attending to the richness of doing everything we need to craft, process, revise, edit and press send for submission and appreciate the journey.

I love so much about this book. It is a book I wish I had had when I began my journey into research, writing, and the academy. It is personable, practical and brings together the theory in a way that resonates with us quickly. What I especially love about this book, is from the very beginning a perusal of the contents has us wanting to dip in and out with a nodding of our heads of 'oh yes, I need that', 'tell me more …', or 'I'm getting ready to sticky-note and underline this section'. We are invited to challenge our guilt or things that embarrass us as we engage with the PhD journey in a gentle way that supports growth. Advice is given to inspire, not to judge or tell you how it must be done. We are guided through a whole cycle of formulating ideas, drafting, writing, editing, polishing, submitting, and resubmitting BUT most importantly how to rest and move at the same time. An intentionality is set for us as we read this book to embody the interconnecting relationship between writing and wellness. An intention is set that wellbeing and self-care are a part of our writing practice, and with this comes a renewed attitude that we can be better writers and better researchers and thus feel better as writers and researchers.

I reflect upon the writing of Elizabeth Gilbert in the book *Big Magic*, which I paraphrase here: spirituality-minded people will often have an awareness around what the universe grants us, and when the outcome isn't what we had thought or wanted, it is the universe letting us know of the outcome we actually needed. This learning moment comes with an awareness and open-mindedness that facilitates a curiosity in what might be. I think about this book series like messages from the universe that we didn't know we needed to know. Reading and engaging with the various books and over a hundred authors to date, opens up the opportunity to shift, resonate, sigh with relief that I am not alone, interrupt, build our capacity to talk about wellbeing and, most importantly, think and put into action ways we can grow, protect and maintain our self-care. Most significantly for me as the series editor, the books published are about interrupting ways of doing things, shifting conversations from behind closed doors to no longer being secrets but to be a part of who we are and what we do. When I approached Katherine to write this book, we talked at length about holistically approaching writing, and I think you will agree with me, she has responded to this vision in a way that allows us all to learn about how to write well, and be well, for writing in ways that are just right for right now in our universe.

I hope you enjoy this book and that you pass on your learnings with your networks.

*Professor Narelle Lemon*
*Series Editor,*
*January 2023*

# Acknowledgements

To the people in my writing communities who have contributed to this book, including my co-authors Andreas Loewe, Inger Mewburn, Shaun Lehmann, Peta Freestone, Liam Connell; to my writing team, particularly Jessamy Gleeson and Emma Curtin; to my wonderful series editor Narelle Lemon and the generous reviewers who helped make this book better; to Vilija Stephens and the Routledge team who turned my manuscript into a book. This book was written in wellbeing communities: I acknowledge my yoga teacher trainers Mei Lai Swan, Noah Mazé, Rocky Heron and Nichol Chase; people who helped keep me moving, particularly Amanda Barbosa; to reading group convenors, including Fi Belcher, Jeanette Fyffe, Tai Peseta, Juliet Lum and Susan Mowbray; Tana Ivanka, who taught me to bind my own research journal; and for people who shared their expertise and experience with me to help make this book more inclusive, including Lauren Pikó, Zara Bain, Meleesha Bardolia, Miranda Gronow, Tess Ryan and Ana Ximena Torres; and to Jellycat, who sat on my desk, and on the many drafts of this book, and purred loudly.

# Introduction

The greatest freedom to build a writing life that suits you often happens at exactly the same time that you feel most uncertain: starting a new research degree or moving from research into 'writing up'. As someone who regularly talks to researchers in these situations, I hear over and over again that students have amazing productivity hacks and strategies that work really well for them, in their bodies, minds, energy and life. But they feel embarrassed or guilty about putting them into practice because other people have it harder, or they have been told there is a correct way to be productive. They feel they must be doing it wrong if they don't spend 9–5 at a desk in strict 'Pomodoro' time boxes, then an hour at the gym. Or they feel guilty that they 'only' worked 9–5, or any other version of why they are doing it wrong and should feel bad.

There is no right way to write, but many good ways. This book celebrates holistic, effective strategies. It also highlights the evidence-based structures and systems that are most likely to support wellbeing. In this book, I will share the strategies that have worked for me to stay as well as possible while writing. I'll also share the techniques of students and colleagues with whom I've worked, and the many thousands of students and writers covered in the research literature who tell similar stories.

You may already have strategies that help you manage the requirements and challenges of writing a PhD thesis, starting from your own place with your own body, family life, brain chemistry, research field, academic background or personality style. This book gives you permission and encouragement (and maybe a few pointers to explore) to set up a writing practice that you can live with and work with.

DOI: 10.4324/9781003307945-1

Writing is not just getting words on a page or spelling them right. Writing is a complex, multi-stage, iterative process, and each stage has different requirements and challenges. All my writing books have had a version of the writing cycle in them—but this book focuses on the whole cycle. Each chapter includes a toolbox of strategies, mindsets, techniques and approaches to help you, as doctoral candidates, start writing and keep writing, in a way that supports your body, heart and mind to be well, and for you to write good words for a PhD that will pass.

## I.1 Bringing your whole self to the desk

When you are writing, you often have the chance to decide when and where you will work. Do you like to get up before dawn? Work 9–5? Stay up till midnight? You can do that. Do you prefer to handwrite, type into a computer, or dictate your first draft into a phone? You can do that. Do you like to work in short bursts, or long stretches? Do you like music playing or total silence? Do you like to work with others or on your own? You can do that. What's more, you can do that differently across each day or for different stages of the project.

There are already lots of excellent books about how to write a thesis and lots of outstanding books about wellbeing, and I'll recommend my favourites. Sometimes PhD writing books have short sections about wellbeing, as my last two doctoral writing books do, with wellbeing presented as the opposite of writing: writing is hard, solitary and painful; wellbeing is soft, social and healing. Wellbeing is something you have to do on top of your writing, to 'balance' it all out. This book encourages you to challenge that mindset.

I was taught to expect writing to be painful, the 'suffering artist' trope. I also ingested a Platonic idea that the mind was separate from the body, and to live the 'life of the mind' meant to ignore my physical and emotional needs as much as possible. Many other people in modern educational systems have been taught the same (Firth 2021, p. 115). And yet, when I started to find space for my feelings, both emotional and physical, my writing got more efficient and more enjoyable.

So this book is about trying something different. In this book, each of the tools for wellbeing is also a writing tool, and every tool for writing is also a wellbeing tool. These are some ways to write that are all about being well, but also about writing well. The tools I give you in this book will help you to be a great writer. After 20 years of personal experience and advising students, I have found that the wellbeing tools don't require any sacrifices in terms of writing quality, in fact, they often improve the writing quality. Writing better and being better are not in competition, they are synergistic.

Of course, there are other things you need to be doing to be well that are beyond writing, and I encourage you to do that. Have hobbies because they are fun, catch up with people because you like them, see your doctor or therapist for your health, move and eat and rest because that makes you feel good. Those are beyond the scope of this book, but that doesn't mean I don't think they matter.

It's also worth pointing out that things that benefit your wellbeing aren't always easy or comfortable. Some days the writing will be hard, uncomfortable or tiring—that's not necessarily a sign that the writing is negatively impacting your wellbeing. In my experience, therapy, doctor's appointments, exercise and self-reflection are also sometimes hard, uncomfortable or tiring, but the end result is being better in body, mind or heart.

Writing is still my job, and I know that I regularly need to write excellent words, and lots of them, fast. I often tackle difficult and painful material, or material that could hurt other people if I handle it clumsily. I spend hours at my computer and in the library. None of us is forced to write these big challenging academic texts—there are lots of other pathways to learn about the world and make it a better place! But we have chosen a life where writing is a big part of what we do, and many of us aspire to careers where writing remains an important aspect of our work. So this is a book about how to thrive while writing, how to thrive as you plan, draft, edit and revise your texts. The book assumes that you are currently doing a PhD and that you might keep writing after you graduate.

This book starts each chapter with a mindfulness exercise to get us into a good headspace. From talking to a colleague, to success visualization, to breathing exercises, we explore different modes of being mindful.

Next, we'll think about the body that is doing the writing. Our brain is not some separate thing in a jar, it's a major organ of our body, and needs to have enough oxygen, hydration, nutrition, and rest to function properly. It can be easy to forget that our hands, neck, eyes, back and legs are part of our writing process too … or at least to ignore them until they start hurting. I'll suggest a range of body practices, from walking or doing the washing up to a good ergonomic set-up.

Third, there are a series of potential tools to try out for making your writing better, making it more efficient to get writing done, or improving the quality of your writing so people will pass it and publish it. Each of these tools is practical and life-changing. I use them myself, and students in my workshops come back later to tell me which technique was a game changer for them. Perhaps some will be a game changer for you.

Finally, bring your own existing wellbeing practices and preferences into how you use this book. You might already have a particular piece of music, or an image, or another ritual to get you into the zone. If you have a physio or personal trainer who has suggested some moves, use those. Maybe there are tools from the many other wonderful writing books that you prefer to the ones I've listed here. Use them! This book gives you joyful permission to find the structure inspiring and then build your own practice. But if you would like to follow some guidelines, there will be step-by-step instructions all the way through.

Why you are writing and how you are getting it done will be influenced by your preferences. Writing has technical aspects, sure. You need skills, and training. And you need to be organized and disciplined about keeping up with deadlines and juggling projects. To gain a PhD, you have to write a lot of excellent, highly polished, rigorous words in a challenging deadline.

But you also bring your weird, inner, non-rational self to the desk when you write. The inner self that has views about what music you can listen to, or which writing rituals you need to do before typing a word. There are good reasons why you might like what you like, but a lot of it is just personal preference, and that is totally a great reason to take it seriously.

It's no one's business how you get your drafts done, as long as you meet deadlines and have polished up your work to be presentable at the end. You are enough, your writing will be enough.

## Notes

Katherine Firth, '5 Ways Hogwarts Helps Us Understand Foucault's 'Docile Bodies'', in Naomi Barnes and Alison Bedford, editors, *Unlocking Social Theory with Popular Culture. Critical Studies of Education*, pp. 113–124. Springer, 2021.

A first version of this section was written for *Research Degree Insiders*: https://researchinsiders.blog/2021/07/08/the-morality-of-writing-well/ and https://researchinsiders.blog/2021/06/10/the-writing-oxygen-and-other-tales-from-inside-a-writing-house/

### I.1.1 Writing with your strengths

I recently ran a writing retreat for early career researchers, and I was surprised at how many of them were privately worried that leaning into their strengths and preferences was somehow cheating at writing. Writing in the way you find easiest is not cheating. Using the support of a writing group or retreat to help you get over the hard bit is not cheating. Working with co-authors is not cheating. (Plagiarism is cheating, everything else is valid writing.) At the same time, nothing makes research writing truly easy. You are creating new knowledge. You are making the unknowable knowable. However efficient or experienced you get, you'll never hack your way to making it effortless. It will always take time.

You should write however works best for you. Morning or night. Together or alone. Voice to text, overwrite, bullet point, edit. Start at the start or the end or the middle. It only matters that you do start. People are experts in themselves. You know what works for you. Own it. Use it. You know what doesn't work for you. Don't use that! It doesn't matter if it works for other people, you do you!

It's helpful iif you also bring this attitude to your co-authors and supervisors. If one supervisor loves line edits and another prefers big-picture thinking, then lean into those strengths for different stages of your work. If you are co-authoring a paper, find out who doesn't mind bashing out a first draft and who loves crafting the footnotes, and give people the jobs they like doing.

At the same time, you need to know what is involved at every stage of the writing process. When you learn more skills or get more experience, some tasks that currently seem impossible will become things you are regularly able to do. PhD candidates love taking on a challenge and learning new things, and you can do that for writing as well as your research.

Keep an eye on the difference between persisting when it's challenging and pushing through to hurting yourself. Sometimes when you think you are done for the day, you can squeeze out another couple of hours of work if you have a nap or join a writing group or go for a walk or have a deadline. It's worth trying. But usually it's good to stop when you still have some energy in the tank (Hemingway 1998, pp. 216–217). Make a note of what you know you need to do next, and then give yourself permission to take a break. It's more important that you come back tomorrow, and the day after.

> **Notes**
>
> Ernest Hemingway, *By-Line: Selected Articles and Dispatches of Four Decades*. Edited by William White. Scribner, 1998.

### *I.1.2 So what actually is writing?*

You've been writing since you were in primary school, and you write every day: emails, grocery lists, text messages, forms. These kinds of writing are generally short and straightforward, and all the multifactorial tasks involved in getting something written can be mixed in together, and you don't have to reflect too much about what you are doing.

Writing a doctoral thesis is different. A thesis is tens of thousands of words, takes years, and explains new and complex information. I might read over a text message once before hitting 'send', but I'd expect to redraft a thesis chapter three or more times before even sharing it with a supervisor.

It's useful to identify the various tasks involved in writing, and then separate them out into distinct focused actions to reduce the costs of 'task switching'. Research tells us that humans don't multitask, they just switch quickly between tasks. For complex work that requires focus (like research and writing), there is a cost of 'attention residue', a lag of a couple of minutes as our brains detach from the last job and get into the groove of the new job (Leroy 2009; Mark et al. 2008). So it is more effective to identify one job and stick to it for a time (perhaps 25 minutes) and then take a break (of perhaps five minutes) before attempting a different task.

For example, a few years ago, I was working on an article and I only had a couple of hours a week to get it done. I know that it takes me about half an hour to read an article, and a few minutes to make a writing plan from that reading. So on Monday afternoon, I would stay back at work for an hour and try to read two articles and plan what I would write. On Thursday mornings, I ran a 'Shut Up and Write' writing group that went for an hour, so I would try to write a section of the article. If I have done my reading, thinking and planning ahead of time, I know I can push out about 400–600 first-draft words per Pomodoro. (These are my numbers, you might be faster or slower, it doesn't matter, only you know yourself and can plan for your own working pace.)

In this case, reading and planning ahead of time was helpful for being as productive as possible on Thursday mornings. But I also benefitted from the 60 hours between the reading and the writing. In that time, I was also thinking about what I had read and what I planned to write. I might focus on a tricky point I wasn't sure how to make and rehearse it in my head. Or I might just have it vaguely in the back of my mind where it was turning over. This space is essential in any conceptualization of the writing process.

At the pace I write first drafts, you can be sure that they aren't very tidy. I then look at the entire article or chapter and make sure the structure and argument are clear and logical. And then I go through to make sure I've caught all the spelling, grammar and punctuation errors, smoothed out the writing, selected the best words. Finally, I'll get a colleague to read it over and give me feedback, which usually leads to some rewrites before submitting to my editor.

So what are the steps in the writing process? Figure I.1 shows an expansion of a cycle that I have included in previous books, and is now, I think,

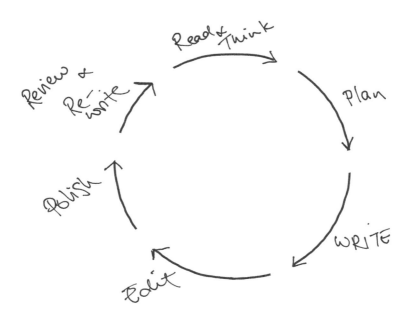

*Figure I.1* The writing cycle

closer to how I explain the cycle when I'm teaching it. Each stage of the cycle is covered in a section of this book, so if you identify a section that you find challenging, you can jump straight to that part of the book for resources. Or you can read the whole book and get a sense of every part of the cycle.

**Read and think:** Writing starts with reading and thinking, and many errors in writing are caused by issues at the reading and thinking stage. If you don't understand a concept, know the vocabulary, or have a logical approach, you won't have good writing. Value the time you spend reading and thinking, and optimize your strategies to help you take those insights into your writing.

**Plan:** Planning encompasses both the practical time and task management aspects of finding time to write, and map out what moves you will be making in your writing. If you find that a list of bullet points and one designated writing day a week isn't helping you to meet your goals, you might find some of the strategies in this section helpful.

**Write:** Writing is when you start with a blank page and put words onto it. It doesn't matter if you do that with a pen, a keyboard, your voice, or any other technique. It only matters that you turn the invisible thoughts in your head into academic prose so they can be read. This is the stage many people find to be the most challenging. Sometimes they try to extend the planning for long enough to jump straight into the editing stage, but unfortunately, you really do need to write something before you can edit it!

**Edit:** Structural editing is a big-picture task. Editing looks at the writing you have done and checks that it is logical, proportional, ordered. When you are editing, you are probably working at the paragraph or section level, checking each paragraph belongs in the draft, and that it is in the right sequence. Are there gaps? Do you have lots of words for important points, and a few words for incidental points? Does the foundational stuff come first?

**Polish:** In creative writing, polishing has two stages: a 'line edit' and a 'copy edit'. Line edits work at the sentence level, making each sentence well crafted. Copy edits are at the word level, identifying spelling, grammar and punctuation errors, and correcting other stylistic details. In academic writing, authors tend to do both of these actions at once, since the writing needs to be functional but not beautiful. The craft of academic writing is in its accuracy, not in its poetry.

**Review and rewrite**: The first time around the writing cycle, you will do the review and rewrite stage yourself. You read over everything you have done, but this time as a reader. Does this make sense? Have you covered everything that needs to be included? You will typically find that you need to go back and read a few more articles, plan a new section, write that section, and rewrite other sections. You will need to check that the structure is still coherent, and then go over it to catch any stray spelling errors and/or unformatted footnotes.

After reviewing and rewriting once or twice, though, this stage will include other readers. Your supervisor will review your work and give you feedback. Usually that involves more research, further thinking, planning and writing or rewriting more material, and then editing and polishing it before resubmitting it for another review.

**Recharge and rest:** You'll notice there is a gap between each arrow in the writing cycle. That's on purpose. Taking a break between the tasks, to recharge and rest, has both wellbeing and cognitive benefits.

Some breaks are about looking after body and soul: maybe you'll refill your water bottle, go to a yoga class, chat to a colleague, or try to get a full night's sleep. This is about preventing hunger, dehydration, back pain, tiredness or boredom from derailing your writing productivity.

But you are also locking in time for your brain to reflect: put things on the back burner, to have a 'critical distance break', to sleep on the problem, to walk far enough away from the project to be able to 'see the forest for the trees'. Any effective writing process needs to have breaks planned to allow for critical distance, task switching, and diffuse thinking.

Thinking about writing as a series of tasks can help us focus on the job at hand and not try to multitask. It also helps us to bring our specific strengths and skills to each of these different stages.

At the beginning of a research project, each stage might reflect weeks or months of work. At other times, each stage might only represent a few minutes of work as we go over things one last time. In the middle, we might find ourselves in helpful loops. For example, you might choose to write up a 500-word chunk of text, structurally edit it, polish it up, and then go back for another 500-word chunk. Once you can see what is involved in actually writing, you can start to intentionally assemble a practice that works for you and for your project.

**Notes**

Sophie Leroy, 'Why Is it So Hard to Do My Work? The Challenge of Attention Residue When Switching Between Work Tasks', *Organizational Behavior and Human Decision Processes*, 109:2, 168–181. 2009.

Gloria Mark, Daniela Gudith and Ulrich Klocke, 'The Cost of Interrupted Work: More Speed and Stress', in *Proceedings of the SIGCHI Conference on Human Factors in Computing Systems*, 107–110. 2008.

The writing cycle has previously been discussed in a simpler form in

Inger Mewburn, Katherine Firth and Shaun Lehmann, *How to Fix Your Academic Writing Trouble: A Practical Guide*, p. 92. Open University Press, 2018.

Katherine Firth, Liam Connell and Peta Freestone, *Your PhD Survival Guide: Planning, Writing, and Succeeding in Your Final Year*. Routledge, p. 112. 2020.

## I.2 Who is doing the writing?

### I.2.1 My story

I grew up in the 1990s. My school, my peers, the adults in my life, my community and popular culture all told me that my body was a problem, my emotions were a problem, and what really mattered was my brain. As a girl, by definition, I needed to be less emotional and not draw attention to my body. A lot of the job interview advice I got was about convincing employers I wasn't about to get pregnant. Of course, I needed to eat and exercise and sleep, but only because otherwise my annoying 'meat sack' would break down and then my brain wouldn't be able to work.

I bounced in and out of being fit, being happy, eating healthily. Sometimes I had everything in a great balance, and sometimes it was all a mess and I'd burn out or injure my back or have week-long migraines. During part of my PhD journey, I had a huge allotment garden where I grew fresh veggies, had a supportive social circle, was active in my local community, and had a regular and productive writing practice. During the last few months of that journey, my allotment was overgrown with weeds, I fell out of touch with my friends, I wasn't getting any exercise or sleeping much. At the end I was exhausted. I completed my PhD in exactly three years, but I didn't have any energy left to turn my research into articles or books or grants.

I could recognize that sometimes I had it right, and that sometimes I wasn't getting it right, but I wasn't really sure how to integrate wellbeing into my researcher life consistently. By this time, I was also teaching and advising students at university, particularly postgraduate students, and it was obvious to me that our bodies, hearts, souls and communities are important parts of making progress on our research. Ignoring our physical, mental, social and emotional wellbeing is clearly a fast route to writer's block, burnout, procrastination or demotivation. It doesn't feel good, and also it doesn't work.

A few years later, I realized that although I had three degrees, two teaching qualifications and extensive professional development in how to manage my time or write a literature review, I didn't have much training in how to rest or move. But I did know how to learn. So I decided to jump in and build up a toolbox of wellbeing strategies that was as comprehensive as my academic skills toolbox.

I asked people what worked for them and tried to take my own good advice. I trained in learning accessibility, as a yoga teacher and as a mental health first aider. I read up on the research, and learned about the diverse ways that people's brains, bodies, cultures and preferences function. I became a supervisor and mentor of doctoral candidates, I ran writing intensives and masterclasses all over the country, I am (sometimes) an academic in a researcher developer team, I write a blog and books about doing a PhD. This helped me to understand why some techniques didn't work for me personally, but they might work for you, and why something else might work for you better.

Having such strategies doesn't stop academic writing being hard, taking work, or requiring time, but it does stop academic writing being detrimental to your wellbeing. Movement, breath and meditation got me through COVID-19 lockdowns while writing three books in two years. Sometimes I have low motivation or feel stuck with a project. Sometimes my back or eyes hurt after a long day in front of my computer. Sometimes I have to navigate complex relationships with co-authors or publishers. Sometimes the world outside (or inside) is terrible. But now I have a toolbox to help me understand what is happening and help me to address it. What's more, getting all of this in alignment means I get to enjoy my writing more, and to use my writing to help spread knowledge and change the world. I would love you to have a toolbox that helps you too.

### I.2.2 Your story

I listen to people like you all the time. I am grateful to all the people who told me their stories, I hope this makes this book useful, inclusive, practical and honest.

You are the expert on your story. You know what strategies and approaches resonate with you, what has worked for you in the past, what your preferences are, your values and hopes, you know who is around you, and who you can rely on to help you out.

---

**Take some time to reflect on your story**

You might like to write down some points in this box.

*If you would like a structured strategy for reflection, try the mindfulness exercise suggested in Section I.3.1.*

---

### I.2.3 It takes a village

Your supervisor or committee are obvious supporters in your academic project, but there are other people in your village: mentors, lab mates, university support staff, conference attendees. And at home: your family, people who care for you or for whom you have caring responsibilities.

But there are also many other communities too. When I was an international student, I lived in a residential college as an undergraduate, and had a part-time job as a graduate student. I joined a choir and reached out to my local faith community. At other times, I have volunteered or found online communities that mattered to me. A big part of my movement practice is having a para-social relationship with my personal trainer and my yoga studio. We invite lots of people over to our house and some of them became part of a found-family. My cat Jelly often sits on my desk and has been an important writing companion.

Take time and be intentional about building your village. Register with a doctor. Find a therapist or a mentor. Seek out a gym where you feel comfortable and are likely to actually go; or use your research skills to find an online movement program that really works for you. Put 'lunch break' as recurring meetings into your diary, and then reach out to people to join you for a sandwich or a midday walk. The time and effort is worth it, to build a sustainable research and writing life—both for your PhD and for the rest of your life.

---

**Notes**

A few recent articles that explore the pleasures and benefits of writing with a community include:

Renaud Le Goix, Myriam Houssay-Holzschuch and Camille Noûs, 'Multiple Binds and Forbidden Pleasures: Writing as Poaching at French Universities', *Environment and Planning A: Economy and Space*, 54:7, 1475–1485. 2022.

Megan McPherson and Narelle Lemon, 'Table Chats: Research Relations and the Impact on Our Wellbeing as Academics', in Narelle Lemon, editor, *Healthy Relationships in Higher Education: Promoting Wellbeing Across Academia*, pp. 132–142. Routledge, 2021.

Cynthia Vincent, Émilie Tremblay-Wragg, Catherine E Déri and Sara Mathieu-Chartier, 'A Multi-Phase Mixed-Method Study Defining Dissertation Writing Enjoyment and Comparing PhD Students Writing in the Company of Others to Those Writing Alone', *Higher Education Research & Development*. Online. 2022.:

---

# I.3 What does 'being well' mean?

Wellness is often used to mean health, happiness, joy or energy, but in this book we take a more holistic approach, a combination of physical, mental, emotional and social health (Eberst 1984). This book doesn't assume you are brimming with strength and resilience and confidence before you can get started or succeed in a research degree. You can take care of yourself, and take care of your writing, whatever your life looks like.

Perhaps you feel like your year swings into productivity and then out again. Perhaps you are aware of all the wobbles and adjustments you are constantly having to make. Perhaps sometimes you need to reach out for support. Maybe sometimes you fall off-balance and have to quickly get back up again. This doesn't mean you are 'unbalanced', this is precisely how human bodies and minds *do* balance. Bodies and minds are complex, dynamic things.

You aren't trying to balance like a stack of rocks, you are aiming for balance like a person. You want to develop the skills and confidence and practice to be able to react to wobbly disturbances, safely move out of the position, rest, and safely return. It's dynamic, and probably not much about staying in one place either. You are not a robot! And you are certainly not a robot on a production line, standing in one place doing the same thing over and over again. You use balance to walk, or to move into red-faced, wobbly, topsy-turvy movement, and then roll out of it, and roll back to the desk for another go. Dynamic balance is what enables you to fall out of focus and get right back into it.

It's not an issue if you finish a stint at your desk feeling like you need to have a stretch, go for a walk and have a snack. That's a fantastic balance of focus and self-care. And as I'll show you in the book, you can use the walk and snack time to progress your writing too, in ways that will make your writing better.

Some people tell me they feel pressured to work in unhealthy ways or are made to feel unwelcome in their department, not by supervisors or their university but by their fellow students. As you build your own wellbeing practices, you contribute to a community and a culture of wellbeing for everyone, even as a student. And as you explore ways to be well as a researcher, you will discover support systems and meet others who are also committed to wellbeing. But even if it is just you, Audre Lorde reminds us that fighting for our own wellbeing becomes most urgent when we can't expect others to look after our wellbeing for us (Lorde 1998/2017, pp. 130–133).

But you don't have to wait until things go wrong, or get 'bad enough', to focus on wellbeing in your writing practice. In fact, we will all be better writers and better researchers (and feel better as researchers) if we focus on wellbeing throughout our PhD and research life.

### I.3.1 'But I'm no good at meditation!'

People often tell me they 'can't meditate': 'I tried', they say, 'but I couldn't clear my mind'. You don't have to have a totally empty mind to start meditating (according to the Dalai Lama 2016; Thich Nat Hahn 1975/2020; and Jon Kabbat-Zinn 1995/2013). Moreover, a completely clear mind is certainly not what you need for mindfulness, which is about filling your mind with the present moment and the thing in front of you.

The suggested mindfulness exercises in this book are pretty short and straightforward. They include things like visualizing your goals, simple breathing, or a short gratitude practice. Most people can get the hang of it with a few tries and start to see benefits in a few weeks. The mindfulness practices are also intended to be warm-ups for the main event. You don't want to exhaust your attention, keep enough left for your research.

Experiment until you find the thing that works best for you, or works for you in this moment. You can always swap some of the thinking exercises like going for a walk or lying on the grass instead. If you already have developed a meditation practice, you'll probably recognize some of the exercises and can start to weave in your own favourites to go deeper. But it doesn't matter if you have a formal practice, it matters that the practice works for you.

### I.3.2 'But I'm no good at exercise!'

The physical wellbeing practices are all pretty simple and don't require you to be athletic or skilled. They sometimes involve things like an ergonomic check of your desk set-up or doing the washing up.

I'll always offer options to help make the practice work for your body. You can also adapt the practice to support you where you are; you are the expert on your body. As always, make sure you are addressing any health concerns with a trained professional who can give you individualized advice before undertaking physical practices.

There are so many ways that people's bodies are different, and your body might even be different day-to-day, so you are the expert on what will help you best! Sometimes you'll want to adapt it to make it easier. Other times you might want to make it more energetic, to match where you are that day. I'll recommend options for both.

**Notes**

Richard M Eberst, 'Defining Health: A Multidimensional Model', *Journal of School Health*, 54:3, 99–104. 1984.

As Audre Lorde writes about 'self-care' in 'A Burst of Light: Living with Cancer', it is when you are sick and marginalized that you need to devote energy to your own wellbeing most urgently. See Audre Lorde, *A Burst of Light: And Other Essays*. Ixia Press, 1988/2017. We return to Lorde in Section 7.3.4

For a discussion on ablism, see Nicole Brown and Jennifer Leigh, editors, *Ableism in Academia: Theorising Experiences of Disabilities and Chronic Illnesses in Higher Education*. UCL Press, 2020.

On meditation and mindfulness, see:

Thich Nhat Hanh, *The Miracle of Mindfulness*. Penguin, 1975/2020.

Jon, Kabat-Zinn, *Full Catastrophe Living: Using the Wisdom of Your Body and Mind to Face Stress, Pain, and Illness*. Random House, 1995/2013.

The Dalai Lama, *The Heart of Meditation: Discovering Innermost Awareness*, translated by Jeffrey Hopkins. Shambhala, 2016.

While a clear mind is a higher stage of consciousness in some traditions, such as set out in the Dalai Lama's commentaries on Patrul Rinpoche (1808–1887), *Three Keys Penetrating the Core*, other teachings such as the *Diamond Sutra* (868 CE) warn against believing that one can be taught or attain such clarity.

For an academic overview of mindfulness, see:

Simon B Goldberg, Kevin M Riordan, Shufang Sun and Richard J Davidson, 'The Empirical Status of Mindfulness-Based Interventions: A Systematic Review of 44 Meta-Analyses of Randomized Controlled Trials', *Perspectives on Psychological Science*, 17:1, 108–130, 2022.

A first version of this section was written for *Research Degree Insiders*: https://researchinsiders.blog/2022/01/06/this-year-im-aiming-for-a-dynamic-balance/

## I.4  How to use this book

This book is a mixture of information and activities. You can read them all in order, or you can jump around identifying things that you think you will find useful, or places where you are currently experiencing difficulties. I'll offer further reading, potential next steps, and options within each section so you can customize your own writing journey.

While the chapters sequentially follow the writing cycle, the suggested activities can be done in any order within each chapter. You might want to do a physical practice as a break during your writing. The meditations are often designed to be warm-ups, but there's no reason you couldn't use them to finish off your writing day. You might fall in love with a particular mindfulness or physical practice and want to repurpose it for other stages of the writing process.

The order of chapters assumes that you are starting your writing journey at the beginning: with no literature review, no ideas, and no plan yet. But you might have picked up this book at any other stage of writing your PhD. The beauty of a cycle is you can join at any time and then follow it around until you come back to the place where you began. And then it will be time to go around the cycle again. You will read this book differently at different stages through your PhD and beyond. 'How shall I write?' means something different as you start your first draft, when you need to persist in writing, or when you face your final deadlines. Visualizing your doctoral graduation is different on day one from day 1,095. And if you use this book beyond your PhD, you'll need to choose another goal to visualize!

This book invites you to look at how you might approach your writing rather than giving you a full and exhaustive writing advice guide. Each section takes a wellbeing approach and focuses specifically on wellbeing strategies to help you produce excellent academic writing. Some of the strategies are about playing to your strengths, or making writing tasks easier, or about building a positive writing mindset. I recommend you mix the advice in this book with advice about good writing and wellbeing, from books, experts, peers and your supervisors, as well as other resources about research methods, theory or project management. Throughout the book, I will highlight potential further resources.

The advice given in this book is relevant to higher degree by research students all over the world, in a whole range of degrees, and writing a range of thesis types. However, the language you might use at your university may differ. I use 'PhD' to stand in for all kinds of research degrees including Honours, Master's by Research and Professional Doctorates; 'student' to talk about the person working towards the degree; 'thesis' to talk about the document produced including portfolios and dissertations; 'supervisor' to refer to the academics responsible for guiding your research and writing; and 'examiners' to talk about the readers of the finished document who decide whether or not you have passed. These elements are consistent across the globe, even when we use different names.

A note on the endnotes: I asked myself, in writing this book, 'what kind of referencing would be generous and useful?' Typically in academic writing, we want our references to be efficient and standardized, in ways that make sense to other experts in our discipline. We also want to ensure we avoid plagiarism and establish enough evidence that someone reading our work with suspicion can double-check our claims (see Section 1.3.5). This book sometimes uses other academic research in these ways, and therefore uses standard citation practices. But I was aware that I am drawing across a really wide range of scholarly traditions (from ancient philosophical texts to modern meta-analyses of randomly controlled trials) for a really wide audience, and so I paid attention to my own search strategies and what helped me trace back to the originals in order to deepen or broaden my thinking. This means the notes in each section are sometimes discursive, sometimes include page or line numbers (even though I haven't quoted from the source), and reference online material like my blog in ways that match how we actually find things online.

Much of this book started life on my blog, *Research Degree Insiders*, and I've given links back to the original versions of the posts so you can see how my writing has developed over time and across the drafting process. I have been thinking and drafting in public and in the community for a decade now, as part of my commitment to making the insider experiences of research visible and accessible. I hope this ends up being helpful—and also encourages us all to reflect on how we can make every layer of our academic writing generous to readers.

## I.5 Wellbeing isn't yet another thing to add to your day

Some of you may be coming to this book while everything is going pretty well. You are looking to optimize your experiences and maintain great habits—and the tools will work well for you. Some of you may be coming to this book when things are a struggle—this book is also written for you. Whether it's the time crunch of being a carer or having a full-time job on top of your research, or needing to navigate stress or disabilities, whether it's writing in another language or culture or dealing with conflict in your supervision team, the tools in this book come alongside you with compassion to help you do what you need to do.

This book isn't about adding lots of extra things to do on top of your writing, it's about naming aspects that are all part of the writing, that will help you write better and feel better while writing. You don't need to be well, or any good, to use these practices.

This book might help you take some useless things away from your writing. I have often seen that academia invests enormous amounts of creative energy into developing writing myths, using analytical energy to work out how we fall short of these made-up measurements, using our problem-solving energies to try to address them, and then draining our emotional reserves in feeling despondent for not being superhero writers. What if instead we put that creative, analytical, practical and emotional energy into realistic writing strategies that actually work, that motivate us, and that make us better writers? As a writing coach, I regularly have these conversations with researchers. So, as I've said before, this book tries to capture some of the strategies that people tell me most often work for them.

The practices in this book are great for people with no equipment, no experience, not a lot of time, and no natural talent for meditation, exercise, or writing. You don't have to start out loving writing or being good at it or being well before you can write. This book takes the approach that sometimes we can just not hate writing that much; or that we can write a terrible draft and then learn how to edit it; that we can find ways to write that work around our bodies, brains and lives. And other times we might find joy in writing, we can use our strengths or preferences to find ways to write that make it easier or more enjoyable; and, through rewriting, we can produce excellent theses.

No productivity tools will help you focus indefinitely or under any circumstances. No productivity hack will turn you into a robot. It will be hard for you to focus, however many breathing exercises you try, if you have worked for too long, are in the middle of an emergency, or are being interrupted constantly by children or co-workers. But you can also channel what focus you do have into writing when you can, or not stressing out because you know you have effective strategies for getting back into writing after a break.

Writing well is hard, and being well can be a challenge. But with the right tools, mindset and community, it is absolutely possible. This book outlines some tools, and encourages you to find your own that work even better for your situation. This book is written from a growth mindset, starting with your strengths. And I hope this book enables conversations that help to grow, or help you find, the community of people who support you as we work to make the world a better place through knowing more about it.

Bring your whole self to this book. Use your self-awareness to read this book in a way that is useful for you. If a section seems to be irrelevant, or the advice doesn't sit well with you, that's fine. Set it aside. It might be relevant to you later—the pages will still be there when you need them. Perhaps the section will prompt you to think about ways that you can create a different version of the tool that is perfect for your brain, body, life, or preferences. Perhaps you'll come away with just one or two strategies that turn major hurdles into navigable steps. If the book helps you in any of those ways, I'll be delighted!

So wherever you are, whatever your life looks like, let's explore writing well, and being well, for your PhD, and for the rest of your life.

### Next Steps

To explore writing in the context of care for others, see for example:
James Burford and Genine Hook, 'Curating Care-full Spaces: Doctoral Students Negotiating Study from Home', *Higher Education Research & Development*, 38:7, 1343–1355. 2019.
For more unhelpful myths about what a PhD student 'should' look like, see *Your PhD Survival Guide*, Chapter 5, pp. 59–71.

# Reading and thinking
## Also part of the writing process

Thinking is the first stage of writing. Thinking includes understanding, analysis, creative ideas, problem-solving, conceptualization, and planning. Reading, research, discussions, exploration of the field, taking notes and planning are all 'thinking' tasks. Thinking can also include literally the time it takes to have thoughts—your thinking tasks might look like staring out the window, or going for a walk to mull things over, or fiddling with something else while trying to problem-solve.

Sometimes, we are so keen to 'write every day' or 'write early, write often', that we jump over the important work of reading and thinking. But you won't have a strong argument in your writing if you don't have a clear, logical understanding of what is happening in your data and why. You won't be able to explain a concept you don't yet understand. You won't have the vocabulary and technical terms for phenomena without having read about them and heard about them extensively. For this reason, thinking is not in opposition to writing, but rather the first stage of writing.

Still, thinking is merely the first stage. We can easily stay here in the thinking stage for too long and fail to progress through all the other stages of the writing process. A thesis or a publication must go through every stage of the writing cycle, and more than once, to be completed. Unlike coursework degrees, where you might learn for a few months and only spend a few hours ticking boxes or scribbling down a few sentences in an exam at the end of the course to show your comprehension, a PhD requires you to move into the other stages of the writing earlier and stay there longer.

Thinking can be invisible, or messy, or slow. Thinking can also be instant, explosive, or lucky. Sometimes thinking is procedural, tidy, orderly. All of these are great ways to achieve thinking tasks, and you will probably

DOI: 10.4324/9781003307945-2

experience a mixture of them. It is a mistake to try to avoid the messy, invisible kinds of thinking, or to discount the instant, lucky insights. Similarly, we can discount skim reading or pre-research, but they are valuable forms of reading alongside careful close analysis of texts. Instead, welcome and value all the kinds of thinking and reading.

## 1.1 A mindfulness practice for thinking: Practising focus

There are many ways to learn to focus, but my favourites come from meditation traditions. Meditation is often used in spiritual practices, but it is the same skill we use in the lab or library. Don't worry if you are terrible at it, at first. Learning a new skill is always a bit messy to begin with. Keep it up for a few goes and see if you start to get better.

One of the most basic skills in meditation is to recover from being distracted. Even when there are no external distractions, our mind often wanders off or we get tired or bored. This is absolutely fine, as long as we practice bringing our minds back to the point. Focus is a skill you can learn, and there are some basic steps that can get you started even if you find it challenging to focus sometimes.

This exercise uses a physical object, because it is so much easier to focus on. Any object will do. I have a small rubber duck on my desk which I often use, but anything else would be just as effective!

1. Go to the place you think you would be most likely to do focused work, at the time you plan to be productive. Set up the space so that you could start work immediately, but do not start working just yet. Place the focus object in front of you.
2. Set a timer for two minutes. Breathe slowly and steadily, try to stay calm and relaxed. There won't be a test!
3. Pay close attention to the object. Use your eyes to notice all the details. Do not look away from the object (but do blink!).
4. If you look away, bring your gaze back to the object. You may find it helps to touch the object, or to turn it around. Do this as many times as you need to.
5. When the timer goes off, reflect. What did you notice? Were you able to focus, or was it very difficult? What made it easier to pay attention? Did your focus change over time?

*Figure 1.1* My mindfulness rubber duck

Personally, I find it gets easier to focus the longer I sit with this exercise. The first 30 seconds are a mess, but by the end of the time, I usually feel like I'm entering a calmer mind space. This helps me to know that I can safely ignore the messy start of any work session: if I persist, I will probably reach the zone. Your experience might be different and give you your own insights.

## Options

Many people doing a PhD use a version of this focus practice to help them stay connected to their project: pictures of relevant people above their computers, or a meaningful object from their research, or a scale model on their desk.

Add more senses into your practice, to allow your attention more places to settle. Traditional meditation often uses candles, incense, chanting and strings of beads to support focus. Set up something visual, some scents and sounds, and something to touch. Perhaps describe what you are looking at, out loud, to help you stay connected to the focus object.

## 1.2 A physical wellbeing practice for thinking: A walking practice

In *A Philosophy of Walking*, Frédéric Gros explores ways that walking and thinking are intertwined. Rebecca Solnit in *Wanderlust* and Walter Benjamin in *The Arcades Project* are two of my favourite examples of people walking and thinking through urban spaces. In 'Kinds of Water', the poet Anne Carson walks the pilgrimage trail to Santiago di Compostela, accompanied by epigraphs of Japanese poets. Above Heidelberg University is a beautiful walk called the 'Philosopher's Way', and behind some of the oldest colleges in Cambridge is a walk called 'The Backs'—both places where scholars could jog their thinking by getting physically moving, either alone or in company. We often talk of our thesis, of our career, of our life as a 'journey'.

We can walk to get to places, or we can walk to be between places: with our bodies and our blood and our breath and our brains all in motion. It doesn't matter if you are strolling through beautiful forests, ambling around a city block, walking with a dog or a baby, or pacing around your living room.

Before you set out on your walk, establish the question, problem or task in your mind. Perhaps read an article, look over a draft, or remind yourself of the major points. Then, set an intention for what you will do when you return from your walk. What research will you be tackling when you return? Just have that in mind. Leave yourself a note if it helps.

Now, put all of that out of your mind. You do not need to take it with you. Step away from the research and go for your walk.

As you are walking, notice what is around you. The surface beneath your feet, is it smooth or rough, flat or inclined? Notice the feeling of the air on your skin, is it warm or cool, dry or humid? Notice the smells, whether pleasant or unpleasant. Notice the sounds: voices, bird songs, traffic, music. Lift your eyes up to look at things that are distant, and things that are close. What can you see that is colourful or unusual? What is the sky like today? As you keep walking, you might continue to consciously notice things, or you might let your mind wander to whatever it wants to think about.

As you return from your walk, take a moment to consider what to bring in with you, and what can be left behind. You might leave the rain, other people's dogs, that rehearsed conversation, those meanderings outside. You might remove your shoes or jacket. You might have picked a flower or a feather or a pebble to bring back with you. You might have had an idea or a phrase you want to bring in.

Return to your desk and remind yourself of your question, problem or task. Did it make progress over the walk? Note down any important points. Do you need to tweak your plan after the walk, or are you now ready to dive into it?

In drafting this exercise, I was leading a writing retreat session, and we'd just had lunch, so I felt full and sleepy and not very motivated to get back to my writing. Instead, I set the timer for 25 minutes for everyone, and then threw on a jacket, grabbed my keys and my phone, and walked up my street and back down again, about 18 minutes of walking. The concrete footpath was wide and easy to walk along. It was a warm, humid day, with just a sprinkling of rain, and a cool breeze. I could smell damp soil and exhaust fumes. I heard birds and cars and other people chatting. The sky was grey, but the front gardens were bursting with colourful flowers. Then my mind went to what I was trying to write in this section, and I tried a few versions of things I might want to say. Then I rehearsed an upcoming difficult conversation. Then I thought about my breath, how sticky the weather was, how I needed to replace my walking shoes soon, how delicious my lunch was, how sleepy I had been feeling, how I needed to keep up the fast pace so I wasn't late for the group. When I returned, I quickly jotted down my ideas for what else to say in this section, and then the timer rang.

## Options

Some people tell me that their work commute gives them a place to think between places, so jumping in the car or taking a long bus ride might work for you.

Some people find repetitive physical movement helpful but get bored at a walking pace. If you want a higher-energy outlet, replace the walking with running, cycling, rowing or swimming.

**Notes**

Walter Benjamin, *The Arcades Project*, translated by Howard Eiland and Kevin McLaughlin. Harvard University Press, 1999.

Anne Carson, 'Kinds of Water', in *Plainwater: Essays and Poetry*, pp. 124–187. Vintage, 2000.

Frédéric Gros, *A Philosophy of Walking*, translated by John Howe. Verso Trade, 2014.

Rebecca Solnit, *Wanderlust: A History of Walking*. Penguin, 2001.

# 1.3 How to read and think: Different strategies

The reading and thinking stage is often also where we are at our most creative, exploratory and experimental. For some researchers, you are literally exploring a site or running experiments in a lab. For all researchers, this is the stage where we find out all the ways things don't work. We read a lot of articles that don't turn out to be relevant. Expect failed experiments, dead ends, rabbit holes and tantalizing options beyond the scope of your current project (see Section 7.3.2). These are not wastes of time, they are signs that you are doing truly original work. If we already knew what you were going to find out and how to get there, your work wouldn't be much of a contribution to knowledge.

So thinking is perhaps the stage of the writing process with the most diverse set of tools. You'll have strategies that look like doing nothing, and strategies that look like doing something else, and strategies that look like writing—but they are all part of the amazing knotty challenge of coming to know, coming to analyse, coming to understand.

Every single time I ask a group of researchers about what they do to focus, I'll get a total spectrum of answers. Rather than worrying about what works for other people, reflect on your own personal experience and then start keeping a note of what seems to work and what doesn't. To give yourself options, try to find a few different strategies you can try.

### 1.3.1 Focused versus diffuse mode thinking

I In *A Mind for Numbers*, Barbara Oakley unexpectedly spends very little time explaining how maths works, and a lot of time talking about how brains work. This means her guidance is directly relevant to the mentally challenging task of writing a thesis.

Oakley recommends using three different mental modes to get the most out of your thinking, learning, analysing, problem-solving and recall.

**Preview mode:** Oakley suggests you 'take a "picture walk"' (p. 11) through the chapter or material before you start to dive into the details. This means looking at not only figures, diagrams and illustrations, but also the abstract, title, subtitles and captions. Only then sit down to read and try to understand the content. She writes:

> You will be surprised at how *spending a minute or two glancing ahead before you read in depth will help you organize your thoughts*. You're creating little neural hooks to hand your thinking on, making it easier to grasp the concepts.
>
> (p. 11)

**Focused mode:** Focused mode is the kind of thinking we are most used to considering 'academic work'. You sit down, remove distractions, and purposefully think about something. You use well-known patterns and thinking habits to help you be efficient. You find it is more effective if you have a defined time, place, plan and goal.

Focused work is essential for academic thought. It's also the kind of work we are doing when we are writing and revising drafts. However, it takes a lot of energy and can only be maintained for a limited amount of time. No one is able to go on focusing all day every day. Pay attention to your own attention patterns and plan around them. You are likely to find focused work is easiest when you are most awake and in a setting that supports your focus. That may be early in the morning or late at night: again pay attention to your own attention patterns and plan around them (May 1999).

Focused thinking tends to be logical and linear, so when you run into a roadblock, or need a creative or original approach to a problem, focused thinking can't take you forward. In a PhD, because you are making an original contribution to knowledge, our current mental models can only take us so far. This is the point when we should be moving into diffuse mode.

**Diffuse mode:** Diffuse mode, or resting-state networks, might not sound like useful thinking time. However, diffuse mode thinking is not actually taking a break from thinking. Instead, it's a break from focused thinking. In the background, thinking is still going on (Andrews-Hanna 2012). In this state, you might be better able to get the big picture, to use fuzzy logics, play around, come at a problem from another angle, or be creative (D'Mello et al. 2014; Takeuchi et al. 2011; Wieth and Zacks 2011). Because this thinking mode is closer to resting (and may even include the thinking you do while you are asleep!), you can sustain this kind of thinking for hours, days or even weeks with little effort.

Diffuse mode thinking will probably be taking place whether you want it to or not, throughout your candidature. But it can often be activated intentionally if you notice your brain is getting stuck. I used to go to my community garden and dig potato trenches for a couple of hours every time I got stuck in my writing. I would frequently come back and find that the impossible tangle was easily resolved. Steven King in *On Writing* says that he gets a lot of his best ideas in the shower, while driving or on his daily walk (p. 170): tasks just engaging enough to keep you occupied, but not so difficult that your brain is fully engaged. There's still enough capacity for diffuse mode thinking.

Since good ideas might come to you while you are away from your desk or your hands are full, do make a plan for how you will capture those great insights. Keep a notebook nearby, use the voice memo function on your phone, or use whiteboard markers on your bathroom tiles.

Don't worry if you get back to your desk and find that your great insights don't quite work in your draft. Not every idea you have in the shower will be a major breakthrough, but some of them will be. And you'll have a lot of showers in the years you are working towards your PhD, so there's plenty of time to have another go.

According to Oakley, you should always approach a problem using previewing, then focused thinking, then diffuse thinking, before returning to focused thinking.

## Notes

Jessica R Andrews-Hanna, 'The Brain's Default Network and Its Adaptive Role in Internal Mentation', *The Neuroscientist*, 18:3, 251–270. 2012.

Stephen King, *On Writing: A Memoir of the Craft.* Simon and Schuster, 2000/2010.

Cynthia P May, 'Synchrony Effects in Cognition: The Costs and a Benefit', *Psychonomic Bulletin & Review*, 6, 142–147. 1999.

Sidney D'Mello, Blair Lehman, Reinhard Pekrun and Art Graesser, 'Confusion Can Be Beneficial for Learning', *Learning and Instruction*, 29, 153–170. 2014.

Barbara A Oakley, *A Mind for Numbers: How to Excel at Math and Science (Even if you Flunked Algebra).* TarcherPerigee, 2014.

Hikaru Takeuchi, Yasuyuki Taki, Hiroshi Hashizume, Yuko Sassa, Tomomi Nagase, Rui Nouchi and Ryuta Kawashima, 'Failing to Deactivate: The Association Between Brain Activity During a Working Memory Task and Creativity', *Neuroimage*, 55:2, 681–687. 2011.

Mareike B Wieth and Rose T Zacks, 'Time of Day Effects on Problem Solving: When the Non-Optimal is Optimal', *Thinking & Reasoning*, 17:4, 387–401. 2011.

## Next Steps

The walking practice in Section 1.2 uses movement to activate diffuse mode thinking. The walking practice in Section 2.2 is a focused mode exercise.

Sweeping the paths or doing the washing up can be a chance to be totally present (as you will practice in Section 4.2), but they can also be good strategies for activating diffuse mode thinking.

See more on how to plan your time to match your focus energy in Chapter 2, especially Sections 2.3.1 and 2.3.2. You'll also see these ideas return in Chapters 3 and 4 when we contrast the work of writing a first draft with the recharging strategies.

### 1.3.2 Pre-research reading

Lots of reading, understanding and thinking needs to happen before you get down to the next stage of research. I call this 'pre-research', and everyone needs to do it as they move into new research territory. Pre-research gives you the lay of the land in a new field before you jump into a deeper literature review.

It's common to get a sense of the 'generally agreed' information about a topic using lectures, textbooks, reference books like encyclopedias or dictionaries, or reputable websites. What does 'everyone know'? There have been many times when I have needed a refresher or the equivalent of a week in class, to get my head around the basics of a new topic, perhaps because I'm teaching a class on a new text or I'm working on a field of research that overlaps with another field that I'm more hazy about. Pre-research can give you an easy overview of 'Who, what, where, when, why, how?' to orient you. News articles, podcasts, explainer videos and Wikipedia articles are great ways to learn about a new idea for the first time, even though you would not usually reference them in your literature review.

You can learn a lot about a field by being part of the scholarly conversation, digitally or in person. Talk to your supervisor. Follow academics on social media, go to seminars and conferences, have chats with other people in your department. Pre-research is often a social activity that helps you feel connected to your field. These conversations are essential for your understanding, framing and research planning, even though they won't ever be quoted in your thesis.

There are a lot of reasons why pre-research is unlikely to make it into your final written work. Pre-research is about 'common knowledge', and you don't need a citation for common knowledge. We actually do all know that the sun rises in the east, Tuesday is a day of the week, a metre is 100 cm. Moreover, as common knowledge is settled, pre-research is not where the debate is happening. This is why it was appropriate to quote encyclopedias and dictionaries in your high school essays, since high school is about getting a basic working understanding of the world. Academic writing, however, is a place to put forward arguments and to have debates.

That pre-research gives you a quick primer is a benefit, but it is also a limitation: pre-research is usually quick, and so it is often shallow, perfunctory, or highly condensed. Someone who only had a conversation, went to a lecture or read a Wikipedia article has a very limited understanding of the field. Sometimes that limited amount of information can mean they actually misunderstand the full issue. Even if they are correct, their understanding is not deep and robust enough to stand up to the kinds of scrutiny that we expect of a peer-reviewed article or examined thesis. So while pre-research is a positive and essential stage in your thinking and reading, you can't stay there forever.

Once you have done the pre-research, you are well placed to move on to the next stage of reading. Because of the pre-research, you will probably already have a significant list of the scholarly books and articles that you will cite in your academic writing, and the contexts and concepts needed to understand and analyse them.

---

**Notes**

A first version of this section was written for Research Degree Insiders: https://researchinsiders.blog/2019/01/03/wikipedia-dictionaries-encyclopaedias/ and https://researchinsiders.blog/2019/01/17/how-do-you-get-from-pre-research-to-search-and-then-research/

---

### 1.3.3 Reading the academic literature flexibly and with confidence

A lot of the difficulties that doctoral students have in getting started, in powering through the slow middle, and in getting to completion, are actually caused by reading. So reading well can transform our writing. And you need to keep upskilling your reading throughout the PhD, even if you started out 'good at reading'.

According to Cisco (2020), reading can prompt feelings of being an imposter in graduate students. Students with imposter phenomenon say things like:

> I'm like, 'I really should have known this. ... Am I the only one that doesn't have any inkling what that means?'
> '[I never] completely understand what I read'.
> 'Am I smart enough to pull-out what somebody else would see as important?'

(p. 207)

These students demonstrate that they see reading as an intelligence test (to be fair, they probably learned this from school). As a graduate student, they have been a 'smart' person all their life, but that self-perception is being challenged by their current research. These students also display traits of what we technically call a 'fixed intelligence mindset' (Dweck 2006). People with a fixed mindset see intelligence as an innate characteristic: you are smart or you're not. So if you are failing the reading intelligence test, that would prove you are not smart and certainly not smart enough for a PhD. That *would* be terrifying. Fortunately, it's not true!

Academic intelligence and learning are things you can be taught and you can learn. Realizing and acting in this way is called having a 'growth mindset' (Dweck 2006). If you have a growth mindset, then a text or concept you don't understand is an opportunity to develop, not a judgement on your capacity. If you make a mistake, it's a chance to have another go. In academia, we call this the 'experimental method', and it is the basis of everything we do. The graduate degree is not a test of whether you already know 'this' but a chance to get to know 'this', whatever 'this' might be.

Furthermore, the point of a research degree is to create new knowledge. To do that, you need to be curious and experimental. If smart people 'already know that', it's not new knowledge. If 'everyone knows that', it's not a unique contribution.

People who are trying to read perfectly, or feel like an imposter if they read imperfectly, are trying to read like a good student, a well-behaved, passive recipient of great knowledge. But that is not the best way, or even a good, way to read. People often bristle at this kind of statement, but to be clear about my credentials to argue such a potentially shocking idea: I have a PhD in English literature, and my first degree was at Cambridge University where they believed that everyone needed to learn how to read for academic purposes. I have lectured in reading skills for English literature, as well as academic skills, so I'm pretty confident that my reading advice is solid.

So what ways of reading are unhelpful to PhD students?

**It's not helpful to read every text the same way:** As high school students and undergraduates, we are taught to read slowly, closely, carefully. Even in subjects known for their high volume of reading, undergraduates are given the two most useful journal articles already photocopied and a set text they can buy from the university bookshop. You already know the text is important, that's why you were given it. You also know that the texts are limited, there are never more than three or four things to read in a week. So you read them carefully.

You will need to read certain texts carefully for your PhD too: like foundational theory, or for close textual analysis. If you are in a field like maths or science and you miss a single $\Sigma$ or $^2$ in your equation, the whole thing fails to work—or worse, explodes with noxious gases!

But that's not how you need to be reading the majority of your research texts. Most articles and books need to be viewed, but not closely analysed. So don't read like an undergraduate, because you can't. When your supervisor says 'it may be worth your while quickly flicking through this article', it honestly means you should quickly flick through that article.

**You can't avoid missing things out, and that's okay:** It's not a disaster if you miss one tiny thing, or even quite a lot of things. It's a PhD, not a Nobel Prize, as an article by Mullins and Kiley (2002) reminds us. In my previous book, *Your PhD Survival Guide*, we called this fear of missing out 'Just One More Article Syndrome' or JOMA (2021, p. 78); Kearns and Gardiner call it 'Readitis' (2010, p. 12). The examiners are expecting that you will leave some things out and you will miss stuff. You have fewer than 100,000 words in your thesis, which is nothing compared to all knowledge, even to all vaguely relevant knowledge. Your thesis is supposed to make a limited and incremental contribution to your field.

There will be a tiny number of texts you need to go back to later that you didn't think were important at the time. If the article really does matter, your supervisor or examiner will point it out—that's what edits and revisions are for. But even if you have to travel four hours by train and stay overnight returning to an archive, you will waste less time returning to that archive, than if you read every article as if it were your only chance. (A true example from my own PhD!)

**You'll forget some of the things you read:** That's absolutely okay too! Trying to store all that stuff in your head crowds out room for the important cognitive work you need to be doing: making connections, interpretation, problem-solving. No one is storing all this stuff in their heads. You may want some things you use every day committed to memory. But for the rest, use notebooks, index cards, cloud storage, USB sticks, note apps and reference databases.

**Don't think 'skim' reading is cheating:** Anything that gets you closer to finishing is a good thing. Not stuff that's unethical, of course: no mistreatment of animals, exploitation of human subjects, or plagiarism. But a bit of skim reading? Go for it! There is no moral or intellectual value in punishing yourself, and a PhD is challenging enough without adding extra and unnecessary work.

You should be using the index at the back of a book and the contents page. This also goes for digital reading. Get your computer to skim for you by using your computer to search documents for key terms.

The three stages of speed reading are 'previewing', 'spotting' and 'using signposts'. Speed reading is not the same as close reading, just faster. Speed reading doesn't all happen at one speed or one depth. You read the abstract, the subheadings, and picked the contention out of the introduction to get an overview of the text. You whizz along, keeping an eye out for signposts like chapter headings and topic sentences. When you spot something that seems useful, you slow down, you collect what you need, and then move on. If you know Chapter 2 isn't relevant, you should skip it entirely.

The thing that matters in this scholarly kind of reading is that *you*, not the author, are in control of the speed and length of reading. Sometimes I spend two minutes 'reading' a massive 600-page biography and two hours reading a tiny 60-word poem.

To read flexibly and with confidence, I therefore recommend:

- Read like it's an adventure.
- Read promiscuously.
- Read around the text.
- Just read the index.
- Skim read.
- Start with the Wikipedia page and come back and try again.
- Put the text down and come back in ten years.
- Read it really slowly.
- Read it out loud.
- Listen to someone else read it to you.
- Skip to the end.
- Find something else you like and read that instead.
- Read it ten times.
- Only read the introduction.

Different strategies will work for different texts, and for the different reasons you are reading the texts. But every one of these is a valid and useful strategy. I've used them all, regularly.

Reading is as nuanced and flexible a skill as writing. Even though you have been reading for a long time, a PhD will challenge you to develop even further. Give yourself the permission to do it imperfectly, and you will do it better. Seeing academic reading as an experiment, an adventure and a chance to learn new things will make reading more enjoyable, and also set you up for success in your academic future. So please do have a go at growing your reading mindset.

## Notes

Jonathan Cisco, 'Exploring the Connection between Impostor Phenomenon and Postgraduate Students Feeling Academically-Unprepared', *Higher Education Research & Development*, 39:2, 200–214. 2020.

Carol S Dweck, *Mindset: The New Psychology of Success*. Random House, 2006.

Maria Gardiner and Hugh Kearns, *Turbocharge Your Writing: How to Become a Prolific Academic Writer*. ThinkWell, 2010.

Gerry Mullins and Margaret Kiley. '"It's a PhD, Not a Nobel Prize": How Experienced Examiners Assess Research Theses', *Studies in Higher Education*, 27:4, 369–386. 2002.

*Your PhD Survival Guide.* pp. 78–79.

A first version of this section was written for *Research Degree Insiders*: https://researchinsiders.blog/2020/11/26/when-reading-makes-you-feel-like-an-imposter/ and the *Times Higher Education* (2016): https://www.timeshighereducation.com/blog/five-biggest-reading-mistakes-and-how-avoid-them

### 1.3.4 Taking notes

We might take notes for lots of reasons: to keep ourselves occupied in boring meetings, to jog our memory when we are at the supermarket, to encourage ourselves and others, to give instructions. Here I am talking about the kinds of notes we take as a prelude to writing. These notes are most commonly in response to reading, to research, or meetings with your supervisor.

There are a myriad of notebooks, apps and memos to help you take notes. More important than your particular note-taking style is to make sure your notes include all of the following attributes.

**Coordinates:** How will you find this item again? In academic research, this often means the bibliographic reference. But it might include page numbers, line numbers, library call numbers, or DOI hyperlinks. You might also be taking notes about a meeting, your experiments, or on a field trip: so place, time, date and other people in attendance might also be good ways to locate this material again.

**Content:** Notes are distinct from copies. You may need to copy/paste text, and make tracings, transcripts, topographies, measurements, scans, recordings or other data sets, which are only valuable if they are complete and comprehensive. The only time to copy out lots of content verbatim is if the original documents will not be available to us later, perhaps because they are in an archive or you are in a meeting that won't be recorded.

Notes are the opposite, notes are supposed to be partial. They should highlight what is relevant and important, what you are actually going to use for your draft. Taking notes about content might involve highlighting or underlining on the document; or writing or sketching them in your notebook. For much of your literature review, that might only be a few quoted words or facts, or a one-sentence summary.

Rather than leave your content notes as a pile of related thoughts, you should take your notes to the next level by intentionally making space to summarize or synthesize your overview of the content. Notes should also involve your reactions, responses and connections through arrows, marginalia notes or writing down your commentary.

**Key themes:** Tags, index terms and identifying themes are all useful to add into your notes, to help you find your notes again, and to connect material across different entries. You might use a running set of themes emerging from your data to help you define a research question. Or, once you have identified your key themes, you might use key words to keep your notes relevant and tied to the scope of your current research project.

**Tasks:** Research leads to more research tasks. Perhaps you have found a lot of new articles you need to read. Perhaps you have come across a concept or some vocab you don't understand. Maybe you need to review or revise work you have previously completed. Perhaps you have questions you need to ask, or permissions you need to ask for.

The most important task to consider is how to turn your notes into writing. Write a few lines of academic prose to summarize and synthesize the notes, right there on the same page as the notes. These lines might become a topic sentence for the relevant paragraph, or the summary in a literature review.

If I leave this work until I come to write the draft, then I often find I need to re-read the whole paper or data set again to refresh my memory with enough detail and context to be able to analyse it and strategically draw out what is most important and most relevant to my draft. But that defeats the purpose of taking notes in the first place.

Really good notes will hold on, even for years. For example, just before the pandemic, I had some research leave in the UK to visit a library with a lot of resources not available to me in Australia where I live. Not only did the pandemic hit, but scheduling challenges with two other book projects also meant I didn't get back to the chapter until about 18 months later. Because I had taken such careful notes, including all the elements in this section, I was able to pick up where I left off, and produce a closely researched draft full of complex conceptualization and relevant detail. If I had taken more haphazard or less analytical notes, I probably would not have been able to write the chapter until the borders reopened over a year later.

The way I lay out my notes page looks like Figure 1.2, a variation of the Cornell Method of note-taking that I have updated for my use as a researcher (from Owens and Pauk 2013; Mewburn et al. 2021). You should explore to find a similar note-taking strategy that is robust enough to support you through major life disruptions or just the normal time it takes to get a thesis written.

## Notes

You can find earlier versions of this method for undergraduates in
Inger Mewburn, Katherine Firth and Shaun Lehmannm, *Level Up Your Essays: How to Get Better Grades at University*, p. 109. NewSouth, 2021.
A first version of this section was written for The Thesis Whisperer: https://thesiswhisperer.com/2012/12/12/turn-your-notes-into-writing-using-the-cornell-method/ and *Research Degree Insiders*: https://researchinsiders.blog/2017/04/27/turn-your-notes-into-writing-using-the-cornell-method-second-edition/
Ross JQ Owens and Walter Pauk, *How to Study in College*, p. 260. Cengage, 1962/2013.

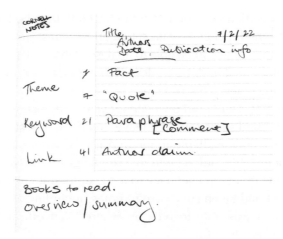

*Figure 1.2* The Cornell Method of note taking adapted for researchers

### 1.3.5 *Generous reading strategies*

Often academic reading is experienced as a chore, or an anxiety, or an extractive industry. You might skim, mine, or categorize your reading. You might read to critique, to look for the gaps. Perhaps you are looking forward to the day when machine-learning tools can do your reading for you. Perhaps you would like to keep up with the wider reading in your field, but don't feel like you have time.

Of course, there are some direct ways that we might find wellbeing in our academic reading. You can find information that offers a solution to a mental, physical or practical problem. It can be affirming to see positive representations of people like you or your work in publications. It can be reassuring to see other scholarship confirming you are on the right track.

But we can also take Eve Kosofsky Sedgwick's 'reparative' reading strategies and think about how to build a generous reading practice. In her chapter in *Touching Feeling* (1997) subtitled 'You're so paranoid, I bet you think this Introduction is about you', Sedgwick sets out a dichotomy of 'paranoid reading' versus 'reparative reading'. Paranoid reading is exactly how we are trained to read as academics. We read with an eye for what is missing, we don't trust anything that is claimed without solid proof. We are looking for reasons to reject articles, we are looking for issues that need resolving in feedback. Doctoral examiners take very seriously the responsibility that they must read theses with what has been called 'a hermeneutic of suspicion' (Ricœur 1965): reading texts with scepticism, doubting the author's intent, looking for places where the author is deluding themselves or concealing weaknesses.

When we are reading to assess, as when we mark, peer review or examine, we are required to use this paranoid reading strategy. 'The examiner doesn't know you and doesn't trust you' is useful basic advice. The purpose of assessment reading is to stop bad things happening in research, so we don't award qualifications to people who shouldn't be trusted. This is essential, *when* it is essential. But we are not always reading for assessment.

When I am reading for academic purposes, sometimes, yes, I am looking for gaps or cracks or issues. But more often, I am reading to understand what other people think, I am looking for interesting ways to tackle a problem, or insightful ways to see a solution. In those cases, paranoid reading strategies don't help much, when I am looking for good stuff.

To start reading from a position of looking for the potential for pleasure has, Sedgwick argues, two implications:

[an] empathetic view of the other as at once good, damaged, integral, and requiring and eliciting love and care [and] … the often very fragile concern to provide the self with pleasure and nourishment in an environment that is perceived as not particularly offering them.

(1997, p. 137)

It is worth noting that at no point does reparative reading assume there are no gaps, no issues, no problems. Instead, it constitutes a relationship between imperfect text and imperfect reader in which 'care' is the defining modality, and for which 'pleasure and nourishment' are the defining goals.

We may have been taught (I certainly was) that to take such a trusting, hopeful, helpful, positive attitude is to be 'sappy' or 'anti-intellectual' (Sedgewick 1997, p. 150). But I have learned to be much more generous as an academic reader through the process of reading with others.

As an academic advisor, writing coach or doctoral supervisor, it's not hard to read student drafts with generosity. They are sitting right there, being nice people, honestly struggling to get their research into writing. I have no trouble being reparative, supportive, helpful, in such circumstances. However, when I am reading the work of senior, established, published scholars, my reading strategies tend to be much more negative.

The best place for me to learn to read positively has been the same place: I need to read with others. Reading with another person also committed to generous reading challenges me to be more positive, and interrupts my negative, un-generous assumptions. So often my negative reactions are gut feelings rather than measured judgements. Being judgemental (rather than judicious) gets in the way of me seeing how scholars from other disciplines or stages of research are able to bring insights that I might miss in my rush to feel sophisticated or expert or—to be honest— clever. When I take a breath and look again, I often find something to value in the writing.

Generous readings don't have to be purely positive readings. Sometimes, as I read generously, I find something that pushes my thinking forward even though I don't agree with it, or it isn't quite how I would approach it. Generosity is about largesse, about expansion, about inclusion. Thinking broadly and openly gives space for better thinking.

At other times, the article is just bad and I hate it, so having someone to share my feelings with helps me to feel better. In this case, reading together is reparative not of the text but of ourselves. Universities are often environments that do not particularly offer care or pleasure or nourishment, but reading with others can make such care possible.

I read-with-others in a number of ways: sometimes with my co-authors, sometimes via Twitter, sometimes with others via my books and blogging. But perhaps the most consistent strategy I've found for generous reading is to belong to an academic reading group. Reading in groups is a great strategy to give you a deadline to get those books and articles out of the 'to be read' pile, and to develop your thinking. Pick a group that matches your time, interests and reading style, or start your own.

Reading can seem like a luxury or a chore in academic life. We need to do our chores, but we can also afford to have our little luxuries, our care of ourselves and of each other.

## Notes

Paul Ricœur, *Freud and Philosophy: An Essay on Interpretation*, translated by Denis Savage, pp. 28–33. Yale University Press, 1965/1970.

Eve Kosofsky Sedgwick, 'Paranoid Reading and Reparative Reading, or, You're So Paranoid, You Probably Think this Essay is About You', in *Touching Feeling*, pp. 123–152. Duke University Press, 1997/2003.

Sedgwick writes her chapter in the context of the HIV crisis, homophobia, racial violence, and her own advanced breast cancer. The joke in Sedgwick's title is a pun on Carly Simon's 1993 hit song, 'You're So Vain, I Bet You Think this Song is About You'.

'Generous reading' tends to be placed in opposition to critical reading, for examples see:

Lucy K Spence, 'Generous Reading: Seeing Students Through Their Writing', *The Reading Teacher*, 63:8, 634–642. 2010.

Kate L Turabian, *A Manual for Writers of Research Papers, Theses, and Dissertations: Chicago Style for Students and Researchers*, 9th edition, p. 39, revised by Wayne C Booth, Gregory G Colomb, Joseph M Williams, Joseph Bizup, William T FitzGerald and the University of Chicago Press editorial staff. University of Chicago Press, 2018.

In contrast, the version of generous reading put forward in this section is also critical and engaged.

## Next Steps

Explore working together through planning in Section 2.4.1 and writing in Section 3.3.3.

Explore reparative strategies through writing in Section 7.3.4 and logical structures in Section 5.3.2.

### 1.3.6 Put aside time to just think

How much time do you have in your typical research day simply for thinking? Not reading or taking notes or going to meetings or organizing data, but giving yourself sustained time to think thoughts? Maybe you only get around to thinking while you are doing other things: like walking the dog or doing chores. These are absolutely times you might have thoughts, but there is a difference between planned thinking time, and just getting lucky while multitasking. Sometimes you need to exclusively think. Not even thinking while you are at your desk or writing your draft or reading a book either, but intentionally and extensively just thinking.

What does thinking look like? Thinking does not 'look' productive. In fact, it can 'look' like doing absolutely nothing. At other times, thinking can appear silly, or boring, or strange, or loud. And so it can be easy to let yourself be convinced that thinking is wasted time. And yet, the most important, original, innovative work in a research project and a writing project is the outcome of your thinking.

It helps if you can schedule your thinking time when you can be alone or you know everyone else will ignore you. Not only does this free you up to think however works best for you, but you also know you aren't interrupting anyone else's thought processes. You might need to move around, talk out loud, stare out the window or close your eyes. You might think better if you are outside, or if you can pace. I avoid thinking tasks in co-working spaces because I make faces and gesticulate; I like loud, upbeat music; and I like to talk my thoughts out loud. Other people make me feel self-conscious, and I know I will be distracting them from their work.

The most important part of thinking is making space for ideas to emerge, to be explored, to be turned over in your head, to be taken apart, to be put back together. One way I like to make space to think is by getting out of the office in nice weather, and sit on the grass. I will start by reading something generative, and then lie back on the grass and stare at the sky for a 25-minute block. I keep a notebook to hand to capture any thoughts, but I try not to use it. The sky is really weird if you stare at it for ages. I let my mind wander. At first, I am itchy and antsy and bored. But as I lie there, my thoughts slow down and open up. In this state, I can be more creative, make new connections, or solve problems. Or I can glom onto a particularly knotty issue and painstakingly pick through it, unravelling it thread by thread.

Sometimes I rise from this time of thinking with the answer, shining in my mind. Sometimes I have tried and discarded a whole raft of dead-ends, which is also important thinking work. Sometimes I have just worked out what the problem actually is. Thinking is like any experiment: it doesn't always succeed, but you won't ever succeed if you don't experiment.

Put time in your diary for thinking. Make space so you can think in the way that is most generative for you. If your thinking time didn't produce amazing new insights, that's not a sign to abandon your thinking practice, it's a sign you still need to do more of it.

---

### Next Steps

If you find that thinking is best activated while doing other things (see Section 1.3.1), you might find the walking practice in Section 1.2 or the mindful washing up in Section 4.2 could be adapted for thinking.

---

### 1.3.7 Journaling

Do you keep a diary? Not a day planner or digital calendar where you schedule in meetings, but a place to record your thoughts and reflect on the day.

If you work in an experimental science field, you may already have a lab notebook: the record of what you did in each experiment, what the results were, why you took those steps, and any new ideas or problems that arose in the research. These are an essential practical, legal and academic record of how you researched. If you are in a field-work discipline, you might similarly keep a record of what you saw, what you found, what you heard, where and when it happened.

It's a good idea for every researcher, in every field, to keep a formal research notebook of this kind. Record your library database search terms that get you the articles you are actually searching for. Record how much you read, or wrote, each day and on what sections of the thesis. Keep a note of who you met at a conference and their contact details. This will be helpful not only for practical reasons, but also for reporting back to your supervisor or annual review of what you did. Tracking your productivity can also help you work out how to plan sensibly for the future in ways that honour your process.

Foucault suggests, in a late lecture about 'Self-Writing', that researchers should use journals 'to capture the already-said, to collect what one has managed to hear or read', not only for the purposes of research but also 'for a purpose that is nothing less than the shaping of the self' (p. 211). The ancient Greek word Foucault uses for notebooks or memoirs (*hupomnēmata*) is closely related to the word for research notebook (*hupomnāmata*). Deliberately bringing together reading with writing through regular reflective practice helps you to construct your own writerly identity, Foucault suggests, which you will later reinforce through going back to your journals and rereading them. It is always a surprise to go back to early notebooks and realize how much you have grown as a researcher, and how much has remained consistent.

Such a journaling and reflective practice can be a form of self-care in another way too. Across the *History of Sexuality*, Foucault returns to a number of ancient Latin and Greek philosophical texts to discuss the 'cultivation of the self' (pp. 48–49). Notably, in *Alcibiades 1*, a dialogue between Socrates and Alcibiades, attributed to Plato, 'self-care' is used to talk about developing expertise and leadership potential, about becoming educated, wise, competent. The focus turns from the management, effort and expertise of the self to self-knowledge in the latter part of the dialogue. This plays on the Delphic motto 'know thyself' (γνῶθι σαυτόν), which Socrates proposes to amend to 'see yourself' (ἰδὲ σαυτόν) through self-reflection, by looking at yourself, as if in a mirror, in order to see your soul or true nature (124b, 132d).

Foucault's ancient sources suggest that we know ourselves, and thus manage ourselves through a daily reflective practice: Seneca says he reflects the morning about the day to come, making his plans and to-do lists, and then, in the evening when things are quiet, undertakes a review of the day (*De Ira* III.36; *Care of the Self* pp. 63–69). But your reflective research journal doesn't have to be updated daily, and it doesn't have to be something you do on your own. Foucault points out in 'Self-Writing' that you can also write your reflections down in 'correspondence' (p. 214). In 2021, I met up every month with a colleague over a video call, and we wrote each other a report on how our writing was going. You might write a version of this report for your supervisor.

Writing your own story is called 'expressive writing' in the literature, and is therapeutic and empowering (Chiew 2021; Wilson 2013). So make space in your journaling practice for looking forward, thinking sideways, being critical and analytical. It's useful to have a place to capture questions about your research, or to express your emotions, or to start to sketch out half-baked ideas. You might keep your expressive writing in the same research notebook, or in a separate place that you keep private.

Record information in all the ways that are useful for you. Do you like to colour code, or keep photographs, voice memos or videos? Do you want to connect information, with arrows or hashtags? Are you using a pencil that might smudge or fade over the next few years? If your journal is online, what are your back-up plans? What will motivate you to actually use the diary?

I love nice paper and pretty pens. I know someone who makes their own research journals with repurposed materials and found images. But it might be more important for your journal to have a waterproof cover or extensive battery life.

Reflective journaling, therefore, can be adapted to whatever you need for your process and your life and your brain and your research, whether you use different strategies across different stages of your research and writing process, or a one-true system across the years. A journal helps you to make your thinking and reading visible, and helps you put it into writing. Articulating your thoughts, the act of writing them down and then of reviewing them later, are powerful research, productivity and wellbeing strategies. They are worth making time for.

## Notes

Examples of research journals include:

'An Idiot's Guide to Fieldwork and Notebooks', UCL Geology Department, n.d. https://www.ucl.ac.uk/earth-sciences-virtualfieldtrip/files/an-idiots-guide-to-fieldwork-and-notebooks.pdf

Philip Ryan, 'Keeping a Lab Notebook Basic Principles and Best Practices', National Institutes of Health, Office of Intramural Training and Education, n.d. https://www.training.nih.gov/assets/Lab_Notebook_508_(new).pdf

*Your PhD Survival Guide*, pp. 52–54. n.d.

There are well-established therapeutic effects for 'expressive' writing, see:

Florence Chiew, 'Writing as Healing', in Paul Crawford and Paul Kadetz, editors, *Palgrave Encyclopedia of the Health Humanities*. Palgrave Macmillan, 2021.

Michel Foucault, *Ethics: Subjectivity and Truth*, Volume 1, edited by Paul Rainbow, translated by Robert Hurley. New York Press, 1997. See 'Self-Writing', pp. 207–222.

Timothy D Wilson, *Redirect: Changing the Stories We Live By*. Penguin, 2011/2013.

The ancient Greek word Foucault uses for notebooks or memoirs (*hupomnēmata*, ὑπομνήματα) is closely related to the word for research notebook (*hupomnāmata*, ὑπομνάματα). See Diogenes Laertius, 'Life of Pythagoras' in *Lives of Eminent Philosophers, Volume II: Books 6–10*, translated by R. D. Hicks, pp. 358–359. Loeb Classical Library 185, 8.1. Harvard University Press, c. 250CE/1925.

Michel Foucault, *History of Sexuality, Care of the Self, Volume 3, Cultivation of the Self*, translated by Robert Hurley. Penguin, 1984/2020.

Plato (attributed), 'Alcibiades 1', in *Charmides. Alcibiades I and II. Hipparchus. The Lovers. Theages. Minos. Epinomis*, translated by WRM Lamb. Loeb Classical Library 201. Harvard University Press, c.390BCE/1927.

Seneca, 'De Ira', in *Moral Essays, Volume I: De Providentia. De Constantia. De Ira. De Clementia*, translated by John W Basore. Loeb Classical Library 214. Harvard University Press, c. 45CE/1928.

## Next Steps

You could use a version of the Cornell Method notes (see Section 1.3.1) to set up your journal, with the side margin and summary sections for making connections and reflection on your research.

We also explore journaling strategies in done lists in Section 2.3.3 and map-making in Section 2.3.4.

## A reflection practice for reading and thinking: Strengths and weaknesses

Now you have read this chapter, it's time to reflect on what you want to take forward and put into practice.

You might use the journaling (see Section 1.3.6), lying on the grass (see Section 1.3.5), or talking to a colleague (see Section 1.3.1) strategies discussed in this chapter as reflection tools. Reflect on the following questions:

- What aspects of reading and thinking are easy for you?
- Which aspects of reading and thinking are hard?
- Which aspects of reading and thinking do you have a lot of experience and skill in?
- Which aspects of reading and thinking are new, or out of practice?

Lean into your strengths (see Section I.1.1) and enjoy this opportunity to grow into areas that currently feel challenging, unfamiliar, or out of practice using a growth mindset (see Section 1.3.2).

# Planning
## Getting to where you want to go

Planning is an essential stage in any project, and particularly useful in a PhD thesis. I used to think of it as part of the thinking stage of the writing cycle, but I realized that it was a distinct, if hopefully short, stage. Planning is helpful before you start to write, but you'll also need to come back to it in the structural edit stage to check that your overall text is meeting your goal and scope.

This section includes two kinds of planning:

1. Time and task management: planning your time so you can get some work done, perhaps by gathering data and conceptualizing how you personally make progress so you can improve your planning.
2. Planning what you are going to write: working out how to make a plan that will productively turn into an excellent thesis and not be an impossible list.

Planning tends to be most effective when you start from a place that is motivating or easy, and you focus on just that one thing. If you distribute your work so that you don't get too exhausted or discouraged carrying it out, you'll also make it easier to come back and do more of it tomorrow (see Section 0.1.1). Managing your energy and motivation can mean knowing how to stop while the momentum is still behind you, or knowing how to rest when you have written yourself into total emptiness.

Planning is future-focused, it's about work we *will* be doing. But we often make our best plans by looking back at what worked best last time. So this chapter also includes advice on tracking your progress and using that to make more realistic plans for next time.

DOI: 10.4324/9781003307945-3

Whatever your situation, your speed, your planning style, whatever motivates you, the planning stage will set you up for being well and writing well more than any other part of this book, which is why this is the longest chapter. Your writing plans will be useful to help you write (Chapter 3) and for your structural edits (Chapter 5) too.

## 2.1 A mindfulness practice for planning: Visualizing your goals

It's easier to get focused when you are doing a task you really enjoy, you are inspired, or it feels like you are definitely going to finish. So this exercise helps you visualize the end of your research to help motivate you, especially if that feels unlikely or distant right now.

1. Go to the place you think you could do focused work, at a time you plan to be productive. Set up the space so that you could start work immediately, but do not start working just yet.
2. Place a sheet of paper in front of you and have a writing implement to hand.
3. Set a timer for two minutes.
4. Take a deep breath in through your nose, and breathe out through your mouth. Then continue to breathe slowly in and out through your nose.
5. Image a moment in the future when you have achieved your doctoral goals. Where are you? What are you doing? Who is there too? How does it feel? Include as many specific details as you can.
6. Write, draw or diagram what this goal looks like and feels like. The lines and words may be representative or abstract, they may be neat or messy, they might make sense to your later self or not. It doesn't matter. Let your pen move over the paper as you imagine that future moment.
7. When the timer goes off, reflect. What did you notice? Did imaging that goal make you happy, motivated and excited?
8. Now get to work for at least 25 minutes. At the end of the session, notice if you were more focused?

Many students tell me they imagine walking across the stage at their graduation, with their family in the audience clapping. They are wearing their doctoral bonnet and the Vice Chancellor shakes their hand. Imagining this movement gives them motivation when the going is hard.

If imaging the future goal made you feel itchy, unhappy or glum, then that is also worth reflecting on. Sometimes I do this exercise and realize I'm having trouble focusing on a task because my brain is sabotaging my productivity to help me escape a horrible future. Maybe you need to change your goals, or your tasks. If that's the case, maybe today isn't the day to get to work, but the day to say 'no' to the project, put things on your not-to-do list, or rethink your priorities.

Either way, visualizing your goals is a powerful tool.

---

### Options

If you have a trusted mentor or friend, you can have a conversation with them. They may want to take notes or just sit and listen. They should give you space to speak for at least two minutes but might prompt you if you get stuck.

As always, if the suggested breathing is distracting or uncomfortable, breathe however works best for you.

---

## 2.2 A physical practice for planning: Stepping yourself through your writing plan

Academic writing consists of a series of 'logical steps' in a 'logical 'order' with no 'gaps'. One way to help yourself plan is by turning those metaphorical steps into physical walking steps.

Start by laying out your plan on the floor. You could use sticky notes, index cards, pages from your draft, figures, or articles you will cite. Arrange the objects into an order that seems logical to you.

Now start walking, following the path you have laid out. It often helps to narrate your walking journey out loud: 'First I will discuss … and that will lead into needing to explain … then I will unpack … finally I will demonstrate …' You might find that this helps you to notice when you say, 'oh, but before I can do that, I really should have explained …' or 'I feel like I'm going in circles here'.

Take one step, then another. Do you have to jump around, shuffle awkwardly, or do you feel lost? Then you need to smooth out your plan. Does your plan feel like a nice walk in the park? Then it's probably ready to write up.

Most PhDs are expected to be linear. If you are doing something non-linear (maybe using a rhizomatic theory, or analysing networks, or using an Indigenous methodology), then you need to clearly signpost what you are doing so your reader doesn't get lost. That narration as you walk the labyrinth of your plan will tell you exactly what your reader needs to know to follow you.

I recommend doing this exercise in a space where you know you won't be disturbed, both to avoid people moving any of your papers until you are ready, and because you might not want to be watched crawling around on the floor and then pacing weirdly around the room!

I first learned this strategy from a fellow PhD student who would go up to the sixth-floor wing of the University Library in Cambridge, one of the corridors where hardly anyone ever went, so he would have the place to himself. He would spread out his rough draft on the floor and then, clicking his fingers, he would walk/dance through the draft. If he could walk it through on the beat, it was right. If he had to double back, if there was a beat missing, he knew there was an issue with his draft.

Turning the steps of your argument into physical steps can help you see the plan more like the way a reader will experience the thesis. The reader will be so grateful if they can follow along your straightforward, well-signposted and danceable pathway!

---

**Options**

Let your fingers do the walking! Create a version of your plan and lay it out on your desk. Using your two fingers, walk through the thesis, narrating it as you go. Does it make sense? Where do you double back or hesitate or jump forward?

---

**Next Steps**

Return to this strategy when you are editing paragraphs to be steps in your argument (see Section 5.3.3).

# 2.3 Time and task management

There are only 24 hours in a day, and seven days in a week. We do not have infinite time. There are, however, infinite things we might do with our time. Doctoral study can go on forever—it was previously common for a thesis to take a decade to write. 'Timely completion' is an external constraint that varies from country to country.

This is a helpful realization. You can never research everything that could be researched, and everyone is just fitting their research and thesis into whatever container their university sets. Rather, a PhD demonstrates your ability to manage a really big, multi-year project as an emerging independent scholar, and produce an original contribution to knowledge. So how *do* you manage your time and tasks to manage a really big, multi-year project and do so independently?

An important part of planning is just getting a sense of how long it takes for you to do things, and what things need to be done. As you go around the writing cycles for each chapter of your thesis, you'll slowly build up a sense of how long it takes you to read an article, how many words you can write in a day, how long it takes you to edit. You'll get a sense of how your supervisor likes to work, and how your writing fits in alongside your research, work, caring and life responsibilities. Then you are able to plan realistically in a way that helps you to write well and be well.

## 2.3.1 Setting your own time and tasks

There is no one ideal way to manage your time and tasks. You need to do enough work, sufficiently frequently to get the work done. If you already know what works for you, go for it!

If you haven't had the luxury and challenge of setting your own working patterns for a while, here's how you can identify some patterns that work for you.

Table 2.1 invites you to reflect on your own preferences for when you like to do focused research or diffuse thinking, when you'd prefer to sleep, recharge and move. But your research may have different pattern requirements, or your life circumstances or other needs may present conflicts. So you will need to compromise your personal preferences with important external factors. Use these categories to work for yourself, your research and your life. The place, or places, where the three preferences overlap are the places where you will be able to get your work done.

Table 2.1 Identify your own working pattern

| Pattern | Focused research | Diffuse thinking | Sleep | Recharge | Movement |
|---|---|---|---|---|---|
| My preference | | | | | |
| Research pattern | | | | | |
| Life pattern | | | | | |
| Other needs | | | | | |

You might prefer to sleep 10.30 pm to 7 am: ., but you are an astronomer and have to work in the middle of the night. Perhaps you are used to working 9–5, but you need to go on site visits, so you cram in some really intensive data collection into a few days, and then have weeks of less intense work as you sort through what you collected. Maybe your hobbies involve a weekly choir rehearsal, but that clashes with a regular seminar at your faculty. Perhaps your preferred movement is ocean swimming, but you currently live a two-hour drive from the sea.

Whatever your situation is, it's helpful to identify each thread of time limitation. This can help you see whether you can manage to have the pattern you prefer at least some of the time, or if there are likely to be changes in your life situation coming up where you could renegotiate so you can work in a way that feels better for you. But also, it can be helpful to see what just isn't going to be your preferred way of working right now and work out what your coping mechanisms are.

Ignore any advice that tells you that you 'must' write every day, or before you start your other work, or you must get eight hours of sleep exactly or you must write in silence or whatever. Don't get hung up on what 'other people' think you 'ought' to do. When I teach time management tools in a workshop, I know there is so much diversity in the ways that different people achieve the same outcome. A PhD is an unusual opportunity to work however suits your brain and life best.

Some parts of our writing work are cognitively hard work. Grappling with new concepts or putting our thoughts into words usually requires intensive focus. You can only work effectively on hard things like writing for a short part of your working week. But there are other parts of the process that might not be so hard. Updating your reference manager, filling out compliance forms, walking between your office and your supervisor's office, and reading university newsletters all take time and are vital, but maybe don't need so much focus.

This is helpful as you plan your time and tasks. Do you schedule your writing when you are most alert and least likely to be interrupted? What other tasks can you schedule into your day at times that match your focus and energy?

I find it helpful to identify both how long a task is likely to take, and how intensive it is likely to be. Giving a presentation, job interviews and academic writing are all very intense for me. I struggle to do more than one of these in a day. However, sitting in meetings, or going to a seminar that someone else is giving is much less intense for me—and it's no issue if I do a lot of these in one day, or balance out some intensive work with some of these less intense tasks.

Email can be a tricky one, because email is a platform, not a task. Some emails are routine and require only a few words of response. Other emails bring tasks that involve hours of work. You can answer some emails quickly on your phone while waiting in line at the supermarket, and other emails require careful thought and half an hour to draft. So perhaps rather than listing 'email' on your to-do list, identify the kinds of work you get in your inbox: approvals, acknowledgements, requests, major projects, and so on.

Working for more than 55 hours each week causes your health and mental abilities to suffer, which negatively impacts your studies, your work, and your home life (Pencavel 2015; Wong et al. 2019). How those hours divide up will be different for everyone, and that's okay, but you need to schedule in time for breaks, for self- and others-care and for fun. Even if you are part of an 'always on' culture, there are ways to manage doing enough good work without burning yourself out. As a graduate researcher, you are probably at the bottom of the pecking order and are unlikely to be able to change an entrenched culture of everyone working ostensibly 80-hour weeks. Because people aren't efficient if they are working that many hours, you might consider 'passing strategies' (Reid 2015) to make sure you look busy even if you are taking a break or caring for yourself. Your productivity will keep track.

Whether you are a part-time or full-time student will make a difference to how you plan your time. However, even full-time does not mean 24/7. You shouldn't be working every hour of the day. Both part-time and full-time students need to plan their research time holistically. What are the various factors you need to plan in?

For full-time students:

- Two to four hours of your best time each day are going to be given to your research.
- You can take part in the wider university and campus culture, such as sitting on leadership committees, going to seminars, joining extra-curricular activities, and chatting to colleagues in the corridor.
- Any outside work you do will be extras to support your time as a student, not the main thing.
- Use 'between times' to add to your student experience.

For part-time students:

- You may need to allocate your best thinking time to other responsibilities. Intentionally carve out space to sometimes give that time to your research.
- What is your first priority? Is it your study? How will you make a decision when a conflict comes up?
- Make time to benefit from campus culture as a part-time student. If you can't often get to your campus during the day, use video-conferencing to attend workshops and seminars, or plan a regular research day on campus.
- Your 'between times' are more likely to be used for connecting to your current job or care situation. Are there ever good moments to connect to your writing or research community?
- Is it best for you to explore leadership and extra-curricular activities in your work or community? Or is the university a better place for this? Perhaps you can have the best of both worlds.

It's comforting to remember that any variation of a sustainable pattern can be made to work, and you'll be okay. It's not necessary to be biohacking your way to optimal sleep protocols or whatever, you can still achieve original research and complete your PhD on time. Human bodies and brains are pretty adaptable, so even if you can't work in your preferred way, it will work out fine.

But feeling confident, motivated and happy are important too. So if you have the choice, choose what you prefer. Writing a PhD thesis is hard enough without adding fake hurdles because of someone else's preferences! If you complete a PhD, writing an original and well-researched thesis, then you get to be called 'Dr', and you'll have earned it, whatever pattern you used to get there.

### Notes

John Pencavel, 'The Productivity of Working Hours', *The Economic Journal*, 125:589, 2052–2076. 2015.

Erin Reid, 'Why Some Men Pretend to Work 80-Hour Weeks', *Harvard Business Review*, 28 April 2015. https://hbr.org/2015/04/why-some-men-pretend-to-work-80-hour-weeks

Kapo Wong, Alan HS Chan and SC Ngan, 'The Effect of Long Working Hours and Overtime on Occupational Health: A Meta-Analysis of Evidence from 1998 to 2018', *International Journal of Environmental Research and Public Health*, 16:12, 2102. 2019.

For more detail on working two to four hours a day or about 20 hours a week on deliberate practice, see:

Brooke N. MacNamara and Megha Maitra, 'The Role of Deliberate Practice in Expert Performance: Revisiting Ericsson, Krampe & Tesch-Römer (1993)', *Royal Society Open Science*, 6:8, 190327. 2019.

A first version of this section was written for *Research Degree Insiders*: https://researchinsiders.blog/2017/03/05/plan-your-research-days/ and https://researchinsiders.blog/2018/08/02/studying-full-time/

### 2.3.2 Writing time 'spreaders' and 'stackers'

Are you a 'spreader', or are you a 'stacker'? Do you prefer to spread out your writing time by writing a little bit every day, or to set aside a 'writing day' and stack up all your writing blocks in one go?

When I talk to writers, the question of how to structure their writing time is one of the most common and also one of the most contested. It's also extremely varied, so whenever I refer to it, it needs some messy phrase like 'your 15 minutes a day' (Bolker 1998) or 'golden hours' (Gardiner and Kearns 2010) or as Helen Sword would call it, your *Air & Light & Time & Space* (2017). But everyone agrees that there is a limited amount of writing energy that has to be distributed across the working week to get a draft written (see Section 2.3.1). So here we are going to use the shorthand terms 'spreaders' and 'stackers' of 'writing blocks'.

A writing block is whatever writing fits in the typical 'time box' you use: whether you prefer to work in 10-minute increments, a Pomodoro of

25 minutes, or something like 90 minutes. I know of at least one academic who would write a few sentences between each student appointment. I don't recommend having a box much longer than two hours, for the sake of your back/eyes/bladder. Between these two extremes, there's a pretty big set of options.

At the end of your block, you might get up for a quick break, and then return for another block, or you might finish writing for the day and go on to other tasks.

You might distribute your boxes across days, weeks or fortnights. Most people aim for between about an hour of writing across the week, up to about 20 hours. This might be based on the time available, or other constraints. Or it might vary depending on where you are in the writing process: for example, in the weeks before submission, most people are writing as much as possible. Whereas, in the experiment or field-work phase, you might just be quickly making notes towards a later draft.

Whether your writing blocks are tiny little mini Lego blocks or great big Duplo blocks, it's now time to decide whether you are going to build something that is spread out, or something that is stacked high. Do note that many of us are neither totally spreaders nor totally stackers, in fact, it's more effective if you do a bit of both!

A spreader prefers to spread their writing across their week. You might try to write for 15 minutes before or after work each day, or get in an hour at least a few days a week. Spreading the writing out makes it feel manageable to you. There's a small amount of it happening a lot of the time, and this means you know you are gradually making regular progress. You never need to worry that the writing is piling up. By spreading it out, you feel you are always on top of the writing.

You might not be a spreader by preference, but spreading might be the best way for you to make progress in your current situation. If you are fitting your writing around other work, have small children, or are living with a chronic illness, there may never be long spaces for you to sit down and work uninterrupted. Learning to be a spreader might make it possible to write your PhD.

Because spreading is adaptable to these kinds of everyday writing circumstances, writing advisers often encourage it. But, like any strategy, it brings benefits and limitations. For example, if you spread things too thin, you may never do enough writing, even though you feel you are always writing. If you only write for five minutes here and there, and it adds up to maybe

20 minutes a day, six days a week, then you feel like you are writing all the time, but added up, it's only a couple of hours in total. That might not be enough to meet your deadlines, especially if you are a full-time student. Make sure your spread adds up to enough writing over the week to make progress.

Another challenge can be spreading out your writing in order to make time for the fact that you are often interrupted, but then you end up not having enough space to focus. The size of your block isn't important, but focus within the block is essential to think new, original, difficult, logical ideas and put them into words!

If spreading can be a good strategy, so can stacking. A stacker prefers to stack up their writing blocks as high as they physically can. You might prefer to put all your writing together with a writing day each week, or a long weekend each fortnight. Stacking the writing all together makes it feel manageable to you. You find a task that spreads out feels messy and uncontrollable, so having it all neatly in one place feels more doable. Or you might find that you are slow to 'get into' the writing, and so you value a longer stretch so you can warm up and really dive deep.

You might not be a stacker by preference, but stacking might be the best way for you to make progress in your current situation. You might work Monday-to-Friday, and so stack all your writing into a Saturday session. Or you might find a writing intensive really helps you to get over the line. Because longer writing events are easier to organize than little writing blocks scattered throughout the day, institutions are more likely to offer writing retreats or intensives.

Again, there can be limitations as well as benefits. For example, if you try to stack the blocks too high, they become unsustainable and unstable. Your body and brain have limits. If you are writing for a long day or two, you will be really tired afterwards. If you write for too long in the day, without enough breaks, your eyes, hands, back and hips will all start to wear out. So pay attention to your stacks and keep them at a height where you know they won't fall over.

Another possible challenge is if you don't get to your stack frequently enough. If you think 'I'll do all my writing in the summer', and then anything else gets in the way of writing (like taking a break, seeing family, getting stuck in your thinking, or getting sick), then your whole stack is endangered. People who don't get to their stack regularly often also find it takes a really long time to get back into writing. It is helpful to get to your writing stack at least once a fortnight, to keep the writing momentum going.

Like playing with Lego or Duplo blocks, there are no limits on the ways you could arrange your blocks, so you don't have to be only a spreader or a stacker. For example, if you go to a couple of 'Shut Up and Write' sessions each week, we could consider that like a couple of spread-out mini-stacks. The possibilities are endless. You might shift your spreading or stacking in different ways across your candidature: perhaps spreading more in phases when you are more focused on researching; perhaps stacking more as you get towards the end.

Many people use both strategies: even within a week, with little writing blocks scattered where you have time and then a full research day once a week; or across the year, like using spreading during the semester, and stacking your writing time in the non-teaching periods. There is no morality, no shame, and no progression between a spread or a stack. Both work well in certain circumstances. It's likely you will do a bit of both sometimes, or move between the two. This is not an immutable personality test, it's a chance to identify your preferences and your practical needs, and use them to help you write and live.

## Notes

Joan Bolker, Writing Your Dissertation in Fifteen Minutes a Day: A Guide to Starting, Revising, and Finishing Your Doctoral Thesis. Holt, 1998.

Maria Gardiner and Hugh Kearns, *Turbocharge Your Writing: How to Become a Prolific Academic Writer*. ThinkWell, 2010.

Helen Sword, *Air & Light & Time & Space*. Harvard University Press, 2017.

Other versions of this strategy are explored in:

Raul Pacheco-Vega, 'Designing and implementing a Publications Planner', 2016b2016a, http://www.raulpacheco.org/2016/06/designing-and-implementing-a-publications-planner/

Robert Boice, *Professors as Writers: A Self-Help Guide to Productive Writing*. New Forums, 1990.

Time boxes are discussed in:

*Academic Writing Trouble*, pp. 8–10; *Level Up your Essays*, pp. 124–25; and *Your PhD Survival Guide*, pp. 39–42.

A first version of this section was written for *Research Degree Insiders*: https://researchinsiders.blog/2017/07/06/moving-beyond-binge-vs-snack-writing/ and https://researchinsiders.blog/2022/06/30/are-you-a-spreader-or-a-stacker/

### 2.3.3 Tracking your progress with 'done lists'

You probably already plan with a to-do list, but we often find that we get to the end of the day and haven't ticked everything off our list. Maybe we planned too ambitiously, or maybe the important tasks that actually got done in the day were different from the morning plan. A solution to this is to use a 'done list', also sometimes called a 'daily résumé' or 'to-done list'. The done list is super simple. At the end of the day, you look back and make a list of all the things you did.

The done list helps you to:

- notice all the things you actually did in the day.
- celebrate the things you achieved and share your successes with others.
- get a sense of what you are able to do in a day or what typically needs doing, thus helping you make better plans for the future.

You don't have to wait until the end of the day to make your done list. Sometimes I make my done list when I'm having a mid-afternoon slump. What have I already done? What is urgent or important and needs doing before I go home? Can I go home on time?

You can write your done list as a list, use an app, or share it on social media for community and accountability. You might want to do your done list as 'the story of my day' or by talking your day over with a colleague. Your done list may be best completed each day, once a week, or once a month.

A done list should hit those lovely reward centres in your brain, so think about what you might find rewarding.

Turning your done list into a rewards chart can be a really fun way to mark progress. Word count might be a good way to reflect your progress, or you might need something more nuanced. Here is an example of how I tracked my productivity towards submitting a co-authored journal article in the summer of 2018 (see Figure 2.1):

- I printed out a calendar from an MS Word template, went to my local big stationary store and bought a lot of little stamps. (I love stationery, so this part was motivating for me!)
- I used a strawberry 🍓 every time I wrote about 500 words.

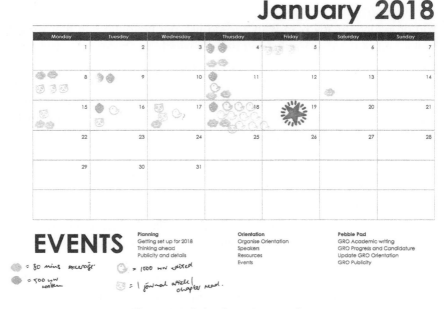

*Figure 2.1* Calendar writing tracker

- But I also needed to edit, and research. So I got a bird 🦆 every time I edited 1,000 words, and a panda 🐼 if I read a chapter or journal article.
- In order to keep myself healthy, I knew I needed to intentionally move, so I got a cloud ☁ if I did 30 minutes of exercise.
- The day before I submitted, the box was full, with a strawberry 🍓, a panda 🐼, some clouds ☁, and 10 birds 🦆 (since I read the whole article one last time). But there were also days I didn't do anything at all towards my research.
- We submitted it on the big star day★.

This rewards chart also helps me to plan for the next time I'm submitting an article, giving me an idea of how much work I should expect to get done, what tasks will come up, and how much time it is likely to take.

You may want to do this kind of tracking every day. Or you may find that you just need to do this from time to time, to get a speed check to keep your planning realistic to where you currently are and to see how fast you are going.

In 2021, I kept a monthly done diary for six months. I wrote 15,000 words in two weeks in early January for upcoming publications; about 1,500 in February; and nothing at all in March. I identified what aspects make up, for me, a 'balanced' and 'good' life, and aspire to have something in each of those baskets each month: like professional development, life admin, catching up with friends, and hobbies. As I've already said, I'm motivated by stationery, so I used a diary with beautiful paper and a really nice pen to reward myself for tracking my progress.

Tracking your progress therefore has benefits in helping you recognize and celebrate what you got done each day, and to plan more effectively for the next time you tackle a similar task. You can use it to share your experiences with others, to activate your rewards, and to feel like maybe you are doing better than you thought.

### Next Steps

A narrative done list might be useful. Try 'The story of my day' using a practice like 'The story of my thesis', outlined in Section 3.1.

You could also try a monthly done diary, or research journal (see Section 1.3.7).

### Notes

A first version of this section was written for *Research Degree Insiders*: https://researchinsiders.blog/2019/01/10/start-making-done-lists-instead-of-to-do-lists/

## 2.3.4 Breaking down a project into smaller steps

How do you break down a big project, set goals and then plan to meet them? Much of the planning advice that is typically given is linear and granular, but in real life, there is so much diversity in how different people achieve their goals.

The first job therefore is to identify your goals. What do you want to achieve, and how will you know if you have achieved it? We are often quite hazy about our far-off-in-the-distance goals, and it can be surprising, but also motivating and reassuring, when we bring them into detailed focus.

For example: do you want a draft that is 'ready to submit' to your supervisor? what does your supervisor consider 'ready'? is that the same for both of your supervisors? Be clear if you actually mean '8,000 highly polished words' or 'all the figures and tables done with bullet points about the planned text'. It is essential to aim for the right thing and know you have got there!

Once you have a goal, there are lots of ways of being productive. Which path you take depends on your preferences, what works for you. I'll explore three styles of being productive that I call 'the step-counter', 'the steeple-chaser' and 'the map-maker'.

**The step-counter:** The step-counter goal-setter likes to have clear, preferably quantifiable, goals, plus the ability to track them. They will be aiming for a daily word count, or to 'close their rings' or 'get in their steps'. They might use writing productivity tracking programs, a count-down ticker, or a word-count tool. They might enjoy super-detailed lists, a bullet journal or writing spreadsheet.

Step-counters find the clarity and granularity of setting and tracking goals to be helpful and motivating. They feel in control and productive if they list out every task, find a time for it in their diary and then tick it off. Because these strategies are often quite linear and documented, they are also often legible to others. PhD supervisors and progress committees often ask for timelines, task lists and Gantt charts as a way to see that you know how to make progress.

If being a step-counter-style project manager is helpful to you, then that's brilliant. Use any of the many productivity strategies recommended in books, workshops or podcasts: pick the ones you like the most.

**The map-maker:** Rather than making a plan by imagining where they are going next, some people find it more helpful to look back over where they have already been, like using an app to record and share your running or cycling route. Rather than using the app like a step-counter, to plan a route and check you are meeting your goals, you can just turn it on and start moving. Over time, you can build up a sense of where you go and how fast you get there. It creates the map from the journey. This kind of planner is going to find reflective tools more useful. Rather than making a to-do list at the beginning of the day, you might try making a done list at the end of the day (Section 2.3.3).

Rather than forecasting your progress and then ensuring that you meet the forecast, you can look back and see if you are on track by the progress you have already made. You know you will get to your goals because you have already mapped similar terrain. Explicitly tracking your typical habits and pacing and ways of getting things done can help you to recognize your progress, and feel secure and motivated to make progress again the next time you need to.

I use both of these styles from time to time, but more often I personally prefer a plan that is simple and flexible, because I'm usually a steeplechaser. If you find the minute detail and focus on counting distracting and stressful, you might find it more useful to have a sense of the big goal, over there, and just head off trying to get there.

**The steeplechaser:** A steeplechase is a kind of cross-country race where you pick a visible landmark (like a tall church spire) and try to get there by whatever way you think is the quickest. There is no fixed route. You can take roads, or go across fields, you might have to jump ditches or climb over fences. You are guessing and improvising a lot of the time, so you might find yourself up to your knees in mud by accident, and then get lucky with a sudden shortcut. Using instincts, information in the moment, and an overall sense of where they need to be and by when, steeplechasers just get there somehow.

For example, I use a whiteboard project planner that only lists the big-picture goals: the project name, the current step in the process and the next deadline. I update the step and dates as I meet each deadline, so it's only ever the next big goal on the whiteboard.

If thinking about the big picture is overwhelming, you can flip it over and think about the smallest first step instead. For example, you could plan only the 'minimum action': something like just sitting at your desk and opening your draft document. In this strategy, just putting on your shoes and turning up for the race is enough. What happens after that is optional. Sometimes nothing much happens. Other times, it means you overcome that initial inertia and are steeplechasing your way towards your bigger goal.

If you have a non-linear or neurodivergent route to meeting goals, this strategy might help you. Circular, stop-and-start, or seemingly distracted paths all eventually get you in the right direction. Ride the productivity flow when it comes, pick the flowers or wander along some intriguing byways when it doesn't.

If you're a steeplechaser, keep the 'ribbons and medals' of completed 'races' somewhere you and your supervisors can see them, reminding you and them that the process may look incoherent or disorganized, but you do keep meeting your goals. Don't waste time feeling guilty if you take a messy or unusual path. There is no approved route, your route gets you there.

In the decade or more that I've been working with doctoral candidates, I have seen thousands of ways to make it to the finish line. It doesn't matter what your style, process or speed is, it only matters that you get there. With a project as long and complex as a PhD thesis, you will need more than one kind of tool. You may need to use different strategies to accommodate team members or institutional guidelines. For example, you might use step-counting to submit a research plan, or map-making to submit a progress report.

I don't think that any particular strategy is more likely to generate productive writers. You can be a careful planner and never meet your goals, a steeplechaser who gets discouraged and gives up, a map-maker who forgets you need to get out there and do stuff before there's anything to look back on. You can miss deadlines and forget tasks regardless of the project management style. You still need to do the work and keep on doing it.

And sometimes life or your health or your head will get in the way, and you can't do the work for a bit. In that case, a done list or Gantt chart is less likely to be useful than your university health service. Whatever your time as a PhD student throws at you, breaking down your project into smaller steps will help you deal with what happens along the way to meeting your goals.

### Notes

Non-linear time planning has been explored increasingly by neurodivergent, gender-diverse and disabled academics. See for example:

Karin Ljuslinder, Katie Ellis and Lotta Vikström, 'Cripping Time – Understanding the Life Course through the Lens of Ableism', *Scandinavian Journal of Disability Research*, 22:1, 35–38. 2020.

Jake Pyne offers a very different travelling metaphor for getting from here to there in, 'Autistic Disruptions, Trans Temporalities: A Narrative "Trap Door" in Time', *South Atlantic Quarterly*, 120:2, 343–361. 1 April 2021.

A first version of this section was written for *Research Degree Insiders*: https://researchinsiders.blog/2021/08/26/how-do-you-break-down-a-big-project-so-you-meet-your-goals/ and https://researchinsiders.blog/2019/01/31/planning-vs-panic-5-strategies-for-success/

> **Next Steps**
>
> For more advice on tracking your progress and setting your pace, especially for step-counter goal setters, see *Your PhD Survival Guide*, Chapter 3, pp. 28–46.

## 2.4 Planning what you are going to write

You will need to submit plans formally for your research proposal and at review milestones through your candidature. You will also need to share plans informally, with your supervisor as you work out what you will cover in the next chapter, or with co-authors as you start to write up research for publications. But don't discount your own, invisible, inside-your-own-head planning techniques like just thinking (see Section 1.3.6).

Some people use something that looks like a plan, but is actually just an *aide-mémoire*, a shorthand reminder of the map they have in their head. The plans I describe in this section aren't bullet-point lists of what will go in each paragraph of the draft. If you use bullet points or lists, the hard bit of writing a thesis (the links and overall structure) is not included in the plan. What's more, planning with a list creates what seems like an obvious logical sequence to your information. But 'list logic' creates descriptive, not analytic, writing. We need 'thesis logic', and you might get feedback that your writing is 'descriptive', 'just a list', 'not theoretical enough', 'not contributing to a cohesive thesis' if you plan your writing using list logics.

The purpose of a thesis is not to list interesting information, the purpose of a thesis is to create a logical academic argument. This section explains how to build narrative and dialogic logics. What's the story of your thesis? Whose research are you responding to? What's your argument? So what?

A good plan motivates you to write, helps you feel confident to write and directs your writing towards your readers and community.

> **Next Steps**
>
> You can jump forward to Section 5.3.2 to find out more about making a logical structure.

### 2.4.1 Dialogical planning

Researchers sometimes discount important work because it's 'just thinking', or 'just chatting', but a good plan that comes out of a productive chat is as valuable as a plan that looks like a list or a calendar. Sometimes these conversations arise informally in corridors or over a cup of coffee, but you can also intentionally use dialogical planning as an important tool in your planning toolbox.

Dialogical planning uses the Socratic method: named after the ancient Greek philosopher Socrates, it's a way of teaching where the teacher asks questions and allows the student to offer the answer. A line of Socratic questioning often starts with a big, open question, like 'why does your research matter?' As you start to answer, the questioner should then respond with further questions raised by your claims, pushing your thinking further. At the end of the dialogue, a skilled questioner will bring you back to their original big open question, and you will find you have an extensive, nuanced and rigorous answer (e.g. Plato, *Theaetetus* 183d–187c).

You might notice that this is a common outcome of a productive meeting with your supervisor. A good supervisor will help you plan your writing by asking good questions, listening to your answers, and then responding to your thoughts. But you can also have informally Socratic conversations with a mentor, another student, or a friend; you can even talk to yourself. You might find it helpful to have a 'written conversation' as if you were writing letters or emails.

Some people always do their best planning through dialogue. If you find that you are super articulate whenever someone asks you a question, but you struggle to explain what you mean when you try to write it down, then recording your dialogical planning sessions might help you to create meaningful outlines for your first draft. Some people process information best by speaking and listening, and find thinking out loud is useful—although your culture and personality is likely to impact if this is true for you (Kim 2002).

But dialogical planning is particularly powerful for everyone in situations where you might need a more flexible or more interactive model of planning.

**When you are trying to find words for what the issue is,** having a conversation can be a fantastic way to move on from 'I have a vague hunch that something is going on here'. By talking it through, you can find words, firm up your ideas, and start to explain or investigate the research question.

**When you need to problem-solve,** workshopping your responses to a problem can be a great way to quickly identify, try out, and discard multiple approaches to the issue. Each approach is a mini-plan. In one half-hour coffee catch-up, you can throw around a range of mini-plans and see if any are useful.

**When the plan needs to involve other people,** brainstorming collaboratively and negotiating proposals with your co-authors, research team or supervisors works well for a project where you all need to be on the same page.

In web design, we often sketch initial plans by hand or use sticky notes on a wall as a way of keeping the plan from looking too finished and thus getting 'set' too early in a project. Sometimes, a really polished-looking plan gets in the way of your writing because it didn't leave enough space for your thinking to evolve as you work through it.

So don't discount the plans that arise from answering questions or talking to a colleague. Intentionally use dialogical planning and capture the incredible insights that arise through dialogue. In time, you will enter 'the conversation' of scholarly debate, you will need to produce a 'discussion' and an 'argument'. These words remind us that our research is about talking to other researchers, questioning them, discussing their work and answering with our own research. A dialogical plan can help us align our first draft with this final goal and with our research community.

### Notes

Heejung S Kim, 'We Talk, Therefore We Think? A Cultural Analysis of the Effect of Talking on Thinking', *Journal of Personality and Social Psychology*, 83:4, 828–842. 2002.

Plato, *Theaetetus. Sophist*, translated by Harold North Fowler. Loeb Classical Library 123. Harvard University Press, c. 369BEC/1921.

To use 'correspondence' for thinking, see Foucault, *Ethics*, p. 214. This is also discussed in Section 1.3.7.

Dialogical planning is not always straightforward, it can be complicated by a range of factors. For example, Das et al. explores a combination of technology, pandemics and neurodivergence with practical advice on how to make dialogue more inclusive:

Maitraye Das, John Tang, Kathryn E Ringland and Anne Marie Piper, 'Towards Accessible Remote Work: Understanding Work-from-Home Practices of Neurodivergent Professionals', in *Proceedings of the ACM on Human-Computer Interaction* 5, CSCW1, Article 183. April 2021.

> ### Next Steps
>
> See Section 3.3.2 for using speaking strategies and software to write your first draft.
>
> Adapt the 'ideal reader' strategy outlined in Section 5.1 to create an imaginary discussion partner.

### 2.4.2 Narrative plans

Your PhD needs to be a coherent body of work, and this coherence is often explained as your 'story'. Stories are how we communicate to each other and remember information. A narrative plan is helpful because you have to keep answering the questions, 'and what comes next?' and 'why?' If you know what comes next and why, you have a really robust logical sequence for your work.

Creative writers have explored a number of ways to plan compelling stories, and we can use their tools to help us produce better academic stories too. Just remember that PhD stories are very straightforward: so avoid cliffhangers, twists in the tale, surprises, jump scares, and too many flashbacks. Keep it linear.

This section recommends two different ways to write a narrative plan. The first strategy lets you tell the story of your thesis in a fun way that plays to your strengths as someone who already enjoys stories. The second strategy produces a narrative plan that looks and sounds more 'academic' and takes you through the process step-by-step. You might use both strategies, or pick the one that speaks to you.

One way to write a more compelling story is to start with an intriguing premise. Creative writers often do this using a 'writing prompt'. This is a stem, or beginning of a sentence, that sends your writing in a particular direction. What would happen if you wrote the plan for your next thesis chapter as a story using one of the following stems?

- 'Once upon a time ...'
- 'No one knew how to get there, until ...'
- 'One day, a mysterious puzzle arrived ...'
- 'You may have heard people say ...'

- 'The older people of the village already knew ...'
- 'It was so unfair!'

Or write your own stem that fits your project better.

Does this stem help you feel inspired to write your draft? Does it explain how everything fits together? Does it feel important and meaningful? Does it feel like other people might want to hear about your story?

If you would like to start with more structure or a more academic tone, you can undertake the following exercise to write a narrative outline for a chapter.

For each of the following 'moves', write a sentence or two to plan your chapter:

1. How will we enter the chapter? You might use a quote, big claim, anecdote, exciting event or other catchy hook opening to engage the reader.
2. Introduce the research object in its context. Write out the name of the main thing you are researching (text, experiment, case study, field trip, social group, piece of technology, etc.). Add any really important features we need to know about it.
3. What is the overall theme of the thesis that will carry throughout all the chapters? How does this chapter relate to the theme?
4. What is the goal of the research object, what is it trying to do?
5. What is the flaw, the thing you need to resolve in the chapter for your argument to work? What makes your research project so difficult it will need a PhD project to solve?
6. What is your goal? How will you get there?
7. What method or critical lens will enable you to critique or analyse this object? How does the lens challenge or push the object in new ways?
8. What antagonists are you dealing with? Who disagrees with your research position?
   Describe your antagonist's views.
   Deal with the problems raised by the antagonist.
   Repeat for as many antagonists as required to keep your case strong and safe.
9. What allies or supporters come alongside your argument? Who is helping you to achieve your research goals?
   Describe your ally's views.
   Deal with the new insights raised by the ally.
   Repeat for as many allies as are useful.

10. What is the conclusion that you want this chapter to achieve? Is it a clear closed conclusion, or an open-ended one? (Will this chapter answer your research question, or does it open up further questions to be discussed in future chapters?)

    Move towards the conclusion.

    Achieve the conclusion.

11. Restate the conclusion in the context of the overall theme.

Do these moves help you feel confident to write your draft? Do they explain how everything fits together? Do they sound scholarly and convincing to your supervisor? Do you feel you have all the pieces?

Using either of these techniques will help you to plan your writing in a way that will make your first draft more coherent and compelling. A good plan will be inspiring and make you want to write the draft. And when you come to structural editing, a good narrative can help you restructure if needed, to continue to tell a compelling research story.

---

### Notes

The narrative structured plan is adapted from a creative writing plan developed by Libbie Hawker, a bestselling novelist of over 30 books, in *Take Off Your Pants! Outline Your Books for Faster, Better Writing*. Running Rabbit Press, 2015.

See also, Lisa Cron, Story Genius: How to Use Brain Science to Go Beyond Outlining and Write a Riveting Novel (Before You Waste Three Years Writing 327 Pages That Go Nowhere). Clarkson Potter, 2016.

---

### Next Steps

You can use storytelling techniques to warm up and start your first draft, such as the generative writing practice, 'The story of my thesis' (see Section 3.1).

You can also look forward to structural editing strategies outlined in Chapter 5.

Another great way to create a narrative plan is to use a 'Tiny Text' strategy like the one described in *How to Fix your Academic Writing Trouble* (2018), pp. 145–148, developed from Barbara Kamler and Pat Thompson, *Writing for Peer Reviewed Journals*. Routledge, 2013. See p. 63.

### 2.4.3 Visual plans

Visual plans are powerful tools for creating a map, overview or chart of your writing. A picture can capture a lot of information and present it in an efficient way. 'A picture is worth a thousand words' and a good picture can help you plan a thousand words of your draft.

If you are putting together figures, charts, graphs, maps, plans, schematics or tables, you are already analysing and structuring your information. In other words, a visual representation of your data is a form of planning. Having already created a visual analysis, you might find you can 'write up the data from the figures' as your chapter plan.

Visual planning tools can include:

- circles, lines, arrows or colours
- columns, grids, a matrix, or a spreadsheet
- arranging index cards or sticky notes
- drawing pictures or outlines
- timelines and calendars
- storyboards, comic strips or pictures.

Visual planning techniques should highlight the important content, and how your ideas relate to one another, and how they progress through the draft. For something as complex as a thesis chapter, you are likely to need multiple images. It would not be uncommon to have five to eight figures or tables in a chapter, each one complex and dense with meaning. So your visual plans are likely to need to cover similar levels of complexity and data.

An example: sticky notes are one great visual planning tool because they force you to break down the big story into smaller chunks, and then they can be arranged in ways that help you show relationships. You can layer them in a stack, from first to last point, set them into columns, or compare and contrast pairs, for example. You might move the sticky notes around, show-ing progression, from planned to drafted to edited, for example (like a Kanban system, see Ohno 1988). Or each time you write a point of your plan into your draft, you could take the sticky note, crumple it up and throw it in the recycling. Some people stick the sticky notes to their desk or a wall, but you can also stick them inside a manila folder and take that with you wherever you write.

Here is a sticky note plan I used for a complicated web project (see Figure 2.2). High-level headings sat on the top of each sticky note stack, with more detailed reminders and headings as we went down. There was also a column (on the right) for issues that I needed to come back and fix.

Because I find it so satisfying to mark a completed task by crumpling up and throwing away each sticky note, I can see my progress through this plan by all the gaps and empty spaces.

*Figure 2.2* Using sticky notes to plan

The plan might not be obvious to an outside viewer, but this image immediately conjured up the text that I needed to write and how I would be putting it together.

Like any good writing plan, the purpose of a visual plan is to help you have an overview of the content, help you to structure your writing, and help you to feel confident and excited to write it down. If it can help you feel a sense of accomplishment as you make progress through your plan, that's even better.

## Notes

For more on Kanban from the person who developed the system, see:
Taiichi Ohno, Toyota Production System: Beyond Large-Scale Production. Productivity Press, 1988.

## Next Steps

You might already be using a visual technique to plan your time and tasks (see, for example, Sections 2.3.1 and 2.3.3). Can you adapt that strategy to help you also plan your writing?

*Level Up Your Essays* has lots of other great strategies for visual planning. See pp. 45–58.

## Reflection practice for planning: Likes and dislikes

Now you have read this chapter, it's time to reflect on what you want to take forward and put into practice.

Reflect on the following questions:

- What aspects of planning do I enjoy? What aspects of planning do I not enjoy?
- Does drawing or talking or telling stories give me joy? What helps me achieve more productive results?
- Do I like breaking tasks down into small, practical pieces? Do I like to be inspired by the big picture? What helps me achieve my goals?
- Do I feel comfortable celebrating my successes? What things do I enjoy doing that would be good rewards?

You might use the visual, narrative or dialogical strategies discussed in this chapter as reflection tools.

# Writing
## Getting the words onto the page

We can use the term 'writing' for the whole writing cycle that contributes towards the finished thesis. But there is a specific moment in the process that is purely 'writing it down': not planning, thinking, making notes, structural or copy editing, not rewriting. Just writing.

For many people, this feels like a moment of truth. When your ideas come out of your data, your head, your gut, or your mouth and onto the page, they sit there in black-and-white. They can be read by others. They can be judged by others. First of all, they will be read and judged by you.

On the one hand, this feeling can lead to procrastination, perhaps putting off the scary work of writing down the words until you feel magically 'ready'. But you might have noticed we are still in the first half of the book—there is so much more writing still to do before your draft is complete, so leaving the initial writing until later can leave you with nowhere near enough time to edit, polish and rewrite.

On the other hand, the realization that there is so much more to do can lead to rushing past the writing to get straight into the editing, polishing and rewriting stages. Ironically, rushing past the writing stage typically leads to very slow and painful progress, leading to you not having produced enough words for a PhD thesis, even though all the words you have written are very well edited.

This is what I have previously called the 'perfect sentence vortex':

> You sit down to write. You read over your notes to work out what you're going to say and check-up a couple of articles. You write a sentence. You check the sentence over, and rearrange it. You enter the full bibliographic details of your quotation, and double check the

DOI: 10.4324/9781003307945-4

format in the MLA Handbook. You change a word. You go back to a third article to check a fact. You change a date. Then you move on to the next sentence. In reading over the notes for the new sentence, you note that 'articulate' would be a better word than 'explains', so you go back to the first sentence and tweak it. Then you repeat.

('Escape from the Perfect Sentence Vortex of Doom' 2017)

Instead, having done your reading, thinking and planning, you should just write, at least for about a 500-word chunk of your draft. After you have just written, you can edit, polish and rewrite.

But this advice is easier to say than to put into practice. So this chapter gives you advice about writing strategies, and also about how to support your energy, emotions and beliefs about writing, which are also important for producing enough first-draft words.

---

**Notes**

To read more about the perfect sentence vortex, see https://researchinsiders. blog/2017/06/27/escape-from-the-perfect-sentence-vortex-of-doom-second-edition/ and *Your PhD Survival Guide*, pp. 114–116.

---

## 3.1 A mindfulness practice for writing: 'The story of my thesis'

This is a writing meditation, a form of spontaneous writing. Robert Boice, in his book *Professors as Writers*, develops André Breton, Dorothea Brande and Peter Elbow's 'experimental', 'effortless', 'free' or sometimes 'automatic' writing into a useful technique for academics. A similar practice is Julia Cameron's 'Morning Pages' from *The Artist's Way*.

Spontaneous and then generative writing techniques are useful in conjunction with more formal writing. For example, Boice recommends starting your daily writing session with five to ten minutes of free writing to overcome writer's block, or to generate 'momentum and ideas … especially if you have problems with perfectionism and low self-confidence that make getting started difficult' (p. 47).

Peter Elbow's (1973) instructions are clearest:

> The idea is simply to write for ten minutes. … Don't stop for anything. Go quickly without rushing. Never stop to look back, to cross something out … to wonder what word or thought to use, to think about what you are doing. If you can't think of a word or spelling, just use a squiggle or else write, 'I can't think of it.' Just put down something.
>
> (p. 1)

It's alright if you start and don't have anything to say yet. Boice gives the example of one of his workshop participants, who wrote:

> I don't really know where to start. This writing does not come easily to me. My mind is blank. What should I write about?
>
> (p. 46)

No one else will ever see this writing, so just keep going. Persist, and the writing will often start to flow.

So how do you start with generative writing?

Get out a new document: whether that's a sheet of printer paper, a page in your notebook, or a new document in your word-processing software. Have a pen, pencil or keyboard to hand. Find a timer and set it for ten minutes.

Today the writing prompt is 'The story of my thesis'.

Now, start to write. What is the story of your thesis? What is its origin, its current situation, its future?

Keep going until the timer goes off.

Well done, you did some writing!

Decide if you need to do anything further with this writing. Did it just help clear out some irrelevant thoughts? Did you download a to-do list or identify a problem? Or did you write a sentence or a few words that you want to transfer into your formal draft?

You might keep the paper in a safe place, or you might throw it away—it's up to you.

## Options

You can write on a computer, with a pen and paper, or using voice-to-text (see Section 3.3.2).

**Notes**

Julia Cameron, *The Artist's Way: A Spiritual Path to Higher Creativity*. Profile, 1992/2020.
Peter Elbow, *Writing Without Teachers*. Oxford University Press, 1973.
This section builds on Robert Boice's 'Spontaneous Writing', in *Professors as Writers*, pp. 41–48.

## 3.2 A physical wellbeing practice for writing: Finding the perfect set-up to write, for now

*As I write the first draft of this section, I am in an online writing group. Someone is in bed with their camera off. Someone is on the sofa. People are alone in a room, or sharing with others. People are drinking water, tea, coffee and chai. People are eating snacks.*

Before you sit down to work at your computer, check in with your task, time, energy, body and mind. What would make your writing five to ten percent more productive? What would make your writing five to ten percent more joyful, luxurious, or comfortable?

This is not a forever plan, just for the next 25 minutes of working.

1. Where could you work?
   Inside or outside? In the office, the library, a café, a study, in your car, in the kitchen?
2. What furniture set-up will be most supportive for the next 25 minutes?
   Desk, sofa, kitchen table, bed, floor?
3. What accessories will be most supportive for the next 25 minutes?
   Cushions, blankets, footstools, lap trays, side tables?
4. What visual aids will be most supportive for the next 25 minutes?
   Lamps, glasses, magnifying glasses, printouts, book stands, extra screens?
5. What hearing aids will be most supportive for the next 25 minutes?
   Headphones, speakers, earplugs, playlists, white noise?
6. What about smells?
   Do you have an oil scent or incense that helps you get in the mood? Maybe the library or café has a good smell. Or would you like more fresh air? Is there something in the room you might want to remove so it doesn't smell?

7. What food and drink will be most supportive for the next 25 minutes? Tea, coffee, soda, water, snacks, chocolate, gum. Do you need a proper meal?

8. What other living beings will be the most supportive for the next 25 minutes?
Is your pet a help? What about the kids or office mates? Does it help to have a virtual room of writing companions or the hubbub of people getting on with their days? Or would an absence of other people help?

9. What temperature will be the most supportive for the next 25 minutes?
Is it time to open or close a window? Turn off the heating or turn on a fan? Throw on a pair of gloves or take off the hoodie?

10. What else will help you feel more physically supported in this space?
Maybe you wish you had some hand cream or a throat pastille or a bathroom break. Maybe the piles of papers are in the wrong place or there are too many empty coffee cups on the desk.

11. Now do it. Move to the place you want to work. Set up the space to support you. Collect everything you need. Remove everything you don't need. Shut doors, open windows, move things around, draw boundaries, welcome things in.

12. Take a deep breath. Settle into your working space. Arrange your body in the furniture, arrange your tools on the working surface. Make any last adjustments, clean your glasses, tilt the angle of your screen, push up your sleeves, take a sip of water. Go.

At the end of the 25 minutes, reassess if there is anything you can change about this plan if you are going to continue writing.

## 3.3 How to write: Different strategies

Here are some ways to think about writing that can be supportive of wellbeing, that play to your strengths, that give you the time and place to write, that take a playful, experimental or growth-mindset approach to writing, and that embed your writing in your body, emotions, preferences and community.

Getting words out of your head and onto the page is the only part that no one else can participate in. Yet that doesn't have to mean you are lonely or unsupported. You can write alongside others, or be connected to a writing community to help motivate you.

### 3.3.1 Some version of the terrible first draft

One frequently recommended way to 'just write' is by just getting out a terrible first draft. You can call it 'the zero draft', Boice calls it 'generative writing' (1990) (discussed in Section 3.1), or Anne Lamott calls it the 'Shitty First Draft' (1994/1995). Although there is good evidence for using this technique, people are often resistant to trying it out. Such terrible first drafts are a paradoxically nuanced writing tool for something that is intentionally terrible.

Some first drafts are actually rubbish and do need to be thrown away. This is not necessarily a bad thing, though. They are still useful for identifying and solving writing problems. Truly terrible first drafts are most likely when you are starting or restarting your academic writing.

For example, you might intentionally choose to produce a terrible first draft for getting back into the writing habit, breaking writer's block, or warming up. The writing meditation at the beginning of this chapter used generative writing techniques to help get the writing going, not necessarily to produce a usable draft. I wouldn't do this for longer than an hour on purpose, but you might find you've spent a few days this way by accident, and it's not the end of the world!

Sometimes the draft isn't good because you needed to clear out a blockage first. This is particularly useful for sections you have put off for too long. There's often a wodge of emotional and intellectual gunk encrusted around it. Putting it onto paper collects and stores the gunk, allowing the chapter to flow more freely. Now all that shit is out of the way, you can write better stuff.

If the draft is really bad, it might be evidence you are not ready to write yet, especially if you are less than six months into a new project. Maybe that whiny voice in the back of your head telling you, 'I should be writing', is wrong this time. You may need to do more research, reading, thinking or planning first.

If a draft isn't working, it might be because you are on the wrong track and need to rethink your plan or approach. It's amazing how your beautiful plan can come undone when you actually start writing.

If you are in a discipline where the analysis is done through the writing, you may need to produce a draft just to have done the thinking-through-writing. This is a significant step, particularly in disciplines where a large part of the intellectual work is about wrestling concepts or information into an academic argument. However, these drafts are often not very good in terms of writing.

If your plans are rarely accurate at predicting what the article or chapter is going to look like, a really rough first draft can help you to know the size and shape of the work. I tend to underestimate how long sections need to be, but I write with a co-author who tends to overestimate how much research needs to be crammed into a single article. We don't know how long our drafts will be from the plan, only when we have written it.

It's common to produce something that is pretty rough, but still has a lot of usable content. The draft still needs editing, polishing and rewriting (of course), but it's a first draft on the right track. About half of the writing work has been done. After some light work, it can be shared with others to see if you are on the right track. If you have a co-author or supervisor who isn't bothered by rough work, you can get feedback before you're too invested in the draft to consider starting again, radically changing direction, or ditching a whole section if you need to.

Unfinished work is more stressful and has a higher cognitive load than a finished draft (Zeigarnik, 1938). Many people find editing easier than writing, and even rewriting is easier because you have something to react to, rather than facing a blank page. So if you can produce a rough draft early on, you will feel more confident about completing the project.

Sometimes, most likely towards the end of a thesis project, your 'terrible first draft' will be a 'not so bad after all draft'. You still need to edit, rewrite, refine, consult, revise, polish, but each step will be easier and faster. As you get more experienced with academic writing genres, you should find this happens more and more. Your first systematic review paper is really hard, your 20th should be much easier!

All of these kinds of terrible first drafts are useful for getting started, making progress, solving problems, being a good colleague, and writing like a researcher. This is one of the most useful, liberating and empowering techniques to help scholars and students to move their work forward, so I encourage you to add this to your repertoire of writing techniques.

## Notes

Robert Boice, *Professors as Writers*, pp. 40–72. 1990.

Anne Lamott, *Bird by Bird: Instructions on Writing and Life*. Anchor, 1994/ 1995, particularly pp. 16–32.

Bluma Zeigarnik, 'On Finished and Unfinished Tasks', in WD Ellis, editor, *A Source Book of Gestalt Psychology*, pp. 300–314. Kegan Paul, 1938.

### Next Steps

Perfectionism, self-doubt or writer's block at this stage often indicate a desire to avoid having to revise and rewrite our work. Chapter 7 offers other mindsets that might help.

If a draft is truly terrible, you can use some of the editing techniques outlined in Chapter 5 to see if you can work out what you should be doing instead, or go back to Chapter 2 and see if you can find a strategy to make a new plan and then write a new draft.

Plan for plenty of time to edit, polish and rewrite. Terrible first drafts often come in a bit of a rush, but editing works best if you can take your time and have lots of breaks (see Chapter 4). Put your editing hat back on after a few hours of terrible first-draft writing to be sure you don't spend weeks producing unusable stuff (see Section 6.1). If you are your own worst critic and delete too much, try being 'your own best critic' (see Section 5.3.1) or try to find a supportive but critical writing mentor who gives good feedback (see Section 7.3.1).

### 3.3.2 Your writing software can support your wellbeing

What is the best writing software? When we spend so much time writing and editing, it's essential that we use tools that support us to be effective. What's more, so many programs now automate research jobs that used to take hours of focused labour: finding secondary literature, accessing archives, formatting references, finding themes in NVivo, making graphs, editing images, running complex equations, formatting documents, finding spelling and grammar issues. Surely there's some software that basically writes the thesis for you? Well, not yet!

That being said, actually it's never been easier to get the ideas in your head out into text. Because there are so many different options, you can think about how your writing software can support your wellbeing, by making your writing easier, or more supportive, or more flexible.

Most of us think about typing as the main way to get words onto the page for a PhD thesis. You might use a laptop for its portability. Or you might type on a desktop computer with multiple screens and a separate keyboard and mouse, which is often supportive for your body. You will probably be using MS Word, LaTeX or Scrivener to organize your information and incorporate the references and notes for your final drafts. However, there is no reason why you have to start in those software packages if they aren't the most supportive for you. For example, researchers commonly use Google Docs for the first drafts of a collaborative document.

You might type on your phone or tablet, especially if you are an avid texter or often get your ideas while sitting on the bus or waiting between meetings. You can use the notes app on your phone. You might find that you have produced a useful paragraph or two in an email to your supervisor. Sometimes I write a first draft as a social media post tapped into a phone app.

If you find that you can explain concepts and arguments more persuasively through speaking, you might use voice-to-text functions. Voice-to-text is also good if you prefer to write hands-free, like if you get your best writing inspirations while driving, or to give your wrists a break. Most phones now have excellent voice-to-text apps, or you can use the 'Dictate' function in word processors. You will need to correct the draft, especially any unusual or technical language, but this is typically a fast and straightforward task.

Many people were trained to write by hand for end-of-school examinations. You may still find that this skill of downloading structured and academic thinking onto a sheet of paper in an hour or so of intense writing is a good way to get a first draft written. Other people find that writing by hand gives them easier and quicker ways to move between writing and drawing, or to use characters that are slow to add in the computer but are fast by hand (such as mathematical symbols or Chinese-language characters), so a handwritten first draft might be logical. You can write the first draft by hand. If your first hand-written draft is quite legible and tidy, you can also make use of Optical Character Recognition. Many tablets now offer this function if you write with a stylus onto the tablet screen, but you can also write on paper and scan the image using your phone scanner. Again, you will need to correct the draft, especially any unusual or technical language, but this is unlikely to slow down the process significantly. If your handwriting is hard for the computer to read, you may need to retype it, but that's a chance for an easy rewrite.

Perhaps you are writing on your reading: annotating PDFs on a tablet, taking structured notes, or adding comments in your reference management database. The summaries and any text that arises in response to your reading and research might get drafted there first (see Section 1.3.4).

Almost all of these formats are moved easily between platforms, a simple 'export', or copy/paste, and suddenly it's all appeared in your thesis! This is why it doesn't really matter what software you use to get the writing down, all of these are excellent options for getting that first draft written.

The hard part of the first draft is the act of putting your research and ideas into academic prose. Whether you do this via a keyboard, touch screen, pen or microphone is irrelevant to the final product. So it's worth exploring different options, and keeping up with technology as it improves, so you can work where and how you write most easily or most productively, navigating around other responsibilities. Of course, you will still need to have put in the time and the motivation, and still need to have done the reading, thinking and planning work—but you can get the writing done.

---

### Next Steps

This section will be obsolete soon, so do keep up with the latest developments. Imagine whatever you wish were possible, it's likely someone else has created it, or is about to.

Of course, these different ways of working are not beholden to modern technology either. For example, bell hooks discusses writing her first drafts long-hand and then reading them aloud in *Remembered Rapture: The Writer at Work* (Henry Holt, 1999, p. 36).

---

### 3.3.3 *Writing with others*

While getting words out of your head and onto the page is something only you can do, you don't have to do it alone. Here are some ways to write with others during your PhD journey.

There are many co-working spaces on campus, whether that's a graduate student office, a carrel in the library, or a café table. It can be helpful to have a sense of people around you, also at work, even in a diffuse way.

Writing with other people can help you to make writing more fun, give you external cues about when to start work and how long to keep working, do it with other people, and break down the thesis task into one writing-meeting-sized chunk.

You can intentionally join a writing group. You could set up a small writing group with some friends, join an official program run by your department, or be part of writing groups that might exist for creative writers or researchers in your city or online. Having a time, a place and a task can be helpful for productivity, as is the sound of people around you tapping their keys and getting on with their writing tasks. It's also useful to have this time set aside—if you are in a meeting with your writing group, you can say no to other tasks and meetings. Many departments also offer multi-day writing retreats or intensives, which can supercharge your productivity.

If you prefer to write alone or in silence, you can still benefit from writing with others in asynchronous ways. If you are co-authoring an article, or presenting drafts for discussion to a supervisor, then you are also writing with other people. You can choose a writing buddy or accountability partner, and meet up periodically to swap drafts. Again, other people are helping you to set deadlines and divide up the task into chunks by coming alongside you to do work that is parallel to yours.

Many writing groups create spaces where people go to complain about writing rather than doing writing. These group sessions are sometimes cathartic, and sometimes toxic. This is not the kind of writing community I'm advocating here. Instead, we should encourage an environment where each of us collaborates on the motivation, time, energy and responsibility of getting words onto the page. We can acknowledge that it can be difficult, but we then encourage each other into actually doing the writing. Once the writing is done, we celebrate each other's achievements, and our own. I encourage you to keep your writing meetings for writing.

*Figure 3.1* Non-human writing companions also count.
This is Jellycat 'helping' me edit this book.

Other people can be powerful supporters when we need to 'just write', and we can be powerful supporters for them to achieve the same result. Whether in-person or online, whether together or asynchronously, we can create active, productive writing communities that enable writing to happen, and celebrate it when it does.

**Notes**

A first version of this section was written for *Research Degree Insiders*: https://researchinsiders.blog/2017/06/14/generative-writing-and-shutupandwrite-second-edition/

**Next Steps**

Working with others is discussed more extensively in 'It takes a village' (see Section I.3).

*Your PhD Survival Guide* has more information if you'd like to know more about how to set up a writing group like a 'Shut Up and Write' group (pp. 125–126) or to find out about what happens at a writing intensive like 'Thesis Boot Camp' (pp. 2–4).

For a long run-down of online options, see Katherine Firth, Tseen Khoo, Debbie Kinsey and Hannah James, 'Virtual Shut Up and Write: Now with Added Video' on *Research Degree Insiders*: https://researchinsiders.blog/2020/03/29/virtual-shut-up-and-write-now-with-added-video/

## *Reflection practice for writing: How to value 'just writing'*

Now you have read this chapter, it's time to reflect on what you want to take forward and put into practice.

Reflect on the following questions:

- What was your word count at the beginning of this writing session? What about at the end? Does the change in the number convey the progress you made on your writing?
- If you were working with an accountability partner, how would you describe how your writing session went?
- Does the way you talk about your writing productivity reflect how you really feel about it? What, in fact, do you really feel about it?

Tracking our progress and having a writing accountability partner can be great reflection tools. See Section 2.3.3 for other ways to track your progress.

# 4 Recharging
# Using rest to help you write

Breaks themselves are essential for resting and recharging. But sometimes you need to take a break as part of the writing process, as a way of getting 'critical distance' from your writing in order to identify what's not yet great about it and how to fix it.

If you are a busy researcher who thinks they don't have time for a hobby, or to exercise, or to sleep, then this chapter is about showing you why these elements should be planned in as part of your working pattern, as tools to help you get your thesis written. Taking a critical distance break looks very much like rest or chores or exercise, but the purpose here is not to relax or get your house clean or get fit, but rather to be able to see your draft clearly, solve problems in your argument or energize you to write for a bit longer. (But they do have great wellbeing side-effects, so take that as a matter of grace!)

> **Notes**
>
> A first version of this section was written for *Research Degree Insiders*: https://researchinsiders.blog/2019/09/12/the-critical-distance-break/

## 4.1 A mindfulness practice for recharging: 'Seeing the forest for the trees'

The English-language proverb 'they can't see the forest for the trees' means that someone is so involved in the details (the trees) that they can't see the

DOI: 10.4324/9781003307945-5

big picture (the forest). As a PhD researcher, you need to spend a lot of time looking at tiny details. Microscopic particles, items of code, codicils, footnotes, referencing databases and commas. Sometimes you need to look at the bigger picture, like when you are editing the thesis as a whole. But the big picture is bigger than that. The big picture is your whole life, your whole community, all human knowledge and beyond, to the whole universe.

This is a meditation exercise for putting your work into context.

Find a comfortable position. Maybe you are seated or lying down. Add any cushions or rugs to support your body. Maybe light a candle or open a window. Add music or white noise or silence.

- Keep your eyes open and look around you. Notice any colours or shapes.
- Listen to the noises of the space around you.
- Touch the floor or the furniture you are sitting on.
- Take a breath in through your nose and see what you can smell.
- Notice your tongue, what can you taste?

This is here. This is now. This is your body, your space, your time. Acknowledge yourself without judgement, this is where you are, and you are welcome.

Cast your mind a little bit wider. Who else is in your building? Acknowledge them without judgement, this is where they are, and they are welcome.

Cast your mind a little bit wider. Who else is in your street or campus or neighbourhood? It may help to imagine them from above, or to follow just one sense, like the sight or sound of people. Acknowledge the people without judgement, this is where they are, and they are welcome.

Cast your mind a little bit wider. Who else is in your city or state or country? Acknowledge them without judgement, this is where they are, and they are welcome.

Cast your mind a little bit wider. Who else is in your world? Maybe you can imagine the whole globe? Acknowledge the people without judgement, this is where they are and they are welcome.

- Now, bring your attention back to your tongue, what can you taste?
- Take a breath in through your nose and see what you can smell.
- Touch the floor or the furniture you are sitting on.
- Listen to the noises of the space around you.
- Look around you, notice any colours or shapes.

From where you are, here and now, but with the awareness of your context of this much bigger picture, bring your mind to your research project.

Often, it is when we see our research from a long way away that we see it most clearly.

Your research might seem relevant and urgent, or small and arcane—either is valuable. Notice without judgement.

You might try this exercise before taking a weekend or some time off. You might also try it as you are coming back to your research after a break, to help you remember the big picture of why you are doing this project and how it fits into the big picture of your life, your community, the world and beyond.

---

**Notes**

For the *Collins Dictionary* definition of 'can't see the wood for the trees', see https://www.collinsdictionary.com/dictionary/english/cant-see-the-wood-for-the-trees.

---

**Options**

If the suggested breathing is distracting or uncomfortable, breathe however works best for you. Or you might find that this visualization technique is helped by adding a more intentional breathing exercise (see Section 5.2).

Sometimes this practice is done as a loving kindness exercise (see Section 7.1), sending wellbeing and safety to each group of people as you imagine them.

## 4.2 A physical well-being practice for recharging: Mindful washing up

When we are planning, we are focused on the future. When we are editing, we are looking back at the past. In his classic book *The Miracle of Mindfulness*, Thich Nhat Hanh points out that we are only alive, in our bodies, in this present moment. It is therefore essential to come into the present and inhabit it if we are to rest and recharge. Take a moment where you don't rehearse what you have already done, or go over everything still to do, and just do one simple small task.

Thich Nhat Hanh teaches:

> While washing the dishes, you might be thinking about the tea afterwards, and so try to get them out of the way as quickly as possible in order to sit and drink tea. But that means that you are incapable of living during the time you are washing the dishes. When you are washing the dishes, washing the dishes must be the most important thing in your life.
>
> (p. 26)

This is not 'washing the dishes in order to have clean dishes', this is choosing to 'wash the dishes in order to wash the dishes' (p. 5).

Notice the cup in your hand. Notice the temperature and feel of the water. Notice the sounds. Notice the smells. Notice how your hands move the cup to wash it, how things are dirty and then clean, soapy and then rinsed. Choose to dry the dishes or mindfully put them to drain.

There, you have been present. What makes this time special is not the beauty or importance of the task, but the fact that we have decided to make this time worthy of our attention and care.

You can choose to go on being mindful. Do each task—eating, drinking, resting—as if it were, at that moment, the most important thing in your life. Or you can find the still point, when you need it, by 'washing the dishes to wash the dishes'.

### Options

Thich Nhat Hanh has lots of examples of when you can be mindful: drinking tea, sweeping a path, planting mustard greens, eating a tangerine and going to the toilet are all memorable examples he uses in *The Miracle of Mindfulness*. But he also advocates for it in difficult circumstances, including protesting injustice or being imprisoned.

> **Notes**
>
> Thich Nhat Hanh, *The Miracle of Mindfulness*. Penguin, 1975/2020.

# 4.3 Recharging: Different strategies

Incorporating recharging strategies into your everyday working pattern is essential for life and survival (see Section 2.3.1, Table 1). There is a short list of things that you do have to do every day for self-care. You do need to sleep; you do need to eat, probably multiple times; you will need to do some hygiene tasks like washing your hands, cleaning your teeth, and cleaning away food scraps. It's good if you can get up and stretch a couple of times a day, and try to get some fresh air and sunlight if you can. Make contact with another human being. That's about it.

Recharging is more than just basic maintenance. It should be an integral part of your writing practice. This chapter is about how to make break-throughs and improve the quality of your writing by intentionally incorpo-rating recharge strategies into your writing practice.

Some people hesitate to put down their writing tools because they are unsure how to pick them up again after a break. So this chapter also offers strategies for returning to work with care.

### 4.3.1 The critical distance break

Critical distance is a well-known idea in sociology and humanities research. Gaining distance is vital when the researcher is 'too close' to the subject to be able to make analytical comments about it (Biesta 2007). You can't be critical without being able to step back and assess a situation.

Whether your PhD research is deeply subjective or highly clinical, you will be immersed in the day-to-day details of your work. You will be enmeshed in 'normal' ways of thinking and operating in your context. You will be right up there at the coal-face of your writing, your notes, your sam-ples, your data, your code, your tables, your themes, your transcripts. But then you will have to step back through analysis, reflection or theory before writing up your research.

Your own researcher identity Is also caught up in the details of your writing: your personal career success or failure, the relationships with your supervisor and other researchers, your sense of yourself doing a 'good job'. You might have deep feelings about your research topic. And this is essential to the research process.

But you also need to be able to look at the bigger picture. How does this compare to other works your peer reviewers or examiners have seen? This idea makes sense to you, but can you get a reader to understand it? How might other researchers use this discovery? How is this work relevant to grant funding bodies' priorities? When you are close to the details, it's hard to get perspective on the bigger picture.

It's hard to make critical judgements about your own work when you are too close to it. 'You can't see the forest for the trees'—you can't get a picture of what the forest looks like when you are walking in it. But if you can get some distance, by standing on a nearby mountain or getting up in a helicopter, then you can start to see the bigger picture. One of the best ways to get that distance from your research is by taking some time away from it.

We know it's difficult to task-switch, going from writing to editing or from creating to critiquing, so you will usually be inefficient at both if you try (see Section 0.1.2). Taking a break is paradoxically the quickest and easiest way to give yourself that critical distance.

A critical distance break is some time off that helps you distance yourself from your writing or thinking. It can be a few hours, overnight, or a two-week holiday. You come back refreshed, with a fresh eye, which makes you less likely to miss mistakes, more able to make new connections or solve problems. Things that were hard to see, or hard to articulate, often fall into place after a critical distance break. This is why sleeping on it, going for a walk, or coming back tomorrow can be really effective strategies to break through writer's block, or to problem-solve thinking.

Giving yourself a critical distance break between tasks means you have time to slightly forget what you thought you were doing. So you start to approach your work as a reader, not a writer. When you have critical distance, you are less likely to be caught up in how it feels to do the writing, so you are more likely to see how good what you wrote actually was. This works both for people who tend to hate their writing, and people who tend to be in love with it. If the reason you can't see straight is because you are exhausted, or stressed, or sick, then the break is also sick leave, a mental health break, a holiday.

A critical distance break can help you:

- be more creative
- approach things from a new angle
- catch more mistakes
- be more efficient
- be more critical
- sound more scholarly
- address your reader
- see the bigger picture
- make connections
- not be so overwhelmed by difficult emotions
- feel in control of your research
- have the energy to have another go
- … and much more!

While it's clearly very useful, in an academic culture where working all the time is valued, taking time off can feel like a career-limiting move. If it was hard to take time to do the invisible work of 'thinking' outlined in Chapter 1, it's even harder to take time to do absolutely nothing! So I often get quite a strong negative reaction when I recommend a mini-break from the thesis for a few days. Answers range from 'I am a hard worker, I don't take breaks' to 'my supervisor would be so frustrated if I took a holiday, I'm already so behind!' And I understand that. I really do. But I also know that there are times when taking a break—a ten-minute walk, a half hour nap, a night at the movies, a long weekend away—can be much more effective than working through.

So instead of saying 'why don't you have a rest', I started to prescribe a critical distance break. This is the kind of break you take that is actually a part of your process. A critical distance break is the time you need to be able to see your work from the outside.

The longer you have, the more effective it will be at getting away from your work. You probably don't need a lot of time for small tasks or small sections of work and getting too far away from your work can be counterproductive while you are working to get immersed in it. However, if it's time for a final structural edit of your entire thesis, it's probably a good idea to take at least a couple of weeks, or you just won't be able to get enough space between you and your draft.

When you are stuck, exhausted, confused, blocked or struggling with any aspect of your research, why not try a short critical distance break? It's one of the most effective tools in my personal toolbox and can be transforming for your draft and your life.

**Notes**

Gert Biesta, 'Bridging the Gap Between Educational Research and Educational Practice: The Need for Critical Distance', *Educational Research and Evaluation*, 13:3, 295–301. 2007.

A first version of this section was written for *Research Degree Insiders*: https://researchinsiders.blog/2019/09/12/the-critical-distance-break/ phdsurvival60-62

**Next Steps**

Return to Section 4.1 for a technique to help you 'see the forest for the trees' in your imagination.

### 4.3.2 Make space to recharge by saying 'no'

If you are going to take time to recharge, you need to plan *not* to do certain things. You need to say no to some things, and put up boundaries around your time and energy. So often people talk about boundaries like they are unfortunate negative limitations, all about saying 'no' and 'no more'. This is one way of considering boundaries or edges, that an edge is an affront, that it should be ignored in pursuit of eternal growth. But there are other ways of thinking about boundaries. For example, as a literary scholar, I work on poetry, and the thing that is precious about a poem is its limitations. You only have a few words, they need to be in a certain order, and the more restrictive the order, the more difficult and therefore prestigious the poetry form is.

Similarly, I think about one of my very favourite kinds of food, the Japanese train-station bento box. Figure 4.1 is a picture I took in Japan as I was taking the Shinkansen from Kyoto to Tokyo, perhaps the best bento box of my life.

*Figure 4.1* The very best bento box I ever had

Each little morsel was perfect, framed by its lacquer-like box and encased in a paper patty. I loved how each piece was arranged to be a complete picture in its own right, with just a tiny sprinkle of finely chopped herbs. And I loved that everything wasn't smushed together as a big meal, but a series of tiny meals. Every food item was deliberate and pretty, and felt like a special treat.

And so it's worth thinking about the daily tasks as quotidian as your train-station snacks. The emails, to-do items, meetings and edits can smear all over your day, there's always more of them. Or you could choose to put them in a frame. Each one is a choice morsel, deliberate and delightful. A thing you do on purpose and savour. Seeing a boundary as putting a positive frame around to-do items helped me enjoy setting them and enjoy having set them. I really love a good box, so I suppose it's no surprise that I often use a version of the time box to set limits on my tasks and frame it with a little pause.

Another aspect of the best bento boxes is the way the items balance. Some bitter items, some salty, some sweetish, some palate-cleansingly bland, some that need chewing on, and some that feel like eating air. If you can arrange your to-do items across the week, each day can be a mix of things, so your palate is less likely to get overwhelmed or bored.

The other aspect I value is how each morsel is framed in beauty. Even before I opened this bento box to see the delightful food inside, I was in love with the box. It was so pretty. I am very motivated by pretty things, so I know that good stationery and a nice plant on my desk goes a long way to making me feel happy about the jobs I need to do. Make your joy part of the pause before a task, and the gap after it.

Sometimes you do just need to have a massive bowl of all-in-together ramen eaten in a hurry. I absolutely have weeks where the boundaries are soupy, and sometimes that can be delicious and nourishing too. But when I have the luxury of choice, I love being able to choose to eat out of a bento box.

Unexpectedly, I've found this attitude to boundaries is infectious. Other people are generally delighted to be part of the general delightfulness of my bento box boundaries. It's a pleasure for them to know when I am available and when I am not. I'm more likely to be cheerful when I'm in the office, which is nice for them. They actively work to protect my boundaries because my boundaries are so attractive and keep my work so enjoyable—which means they get to have a nice time when we work together.

My series editor's email signature promises a 'calm inbox', reading that makes me happy for her, and I enjoy that it gives me permission to answer calmly myself.

What metaphor would help you to change your mindset around setting boundaries? And then experiment with joyful, energizing boundaries. You might be surprised by what a calming, affirming experience it is, and how much other people appreciate it too.

## Notes

For more on the power of poetry's limits, see Christopher Ricks, *The Force of Poetry*. Clarendon Press, 1984/2002.

A first version of this section was written for *Research Degree Insiders*: https://researchinsiders.blog/2021/02/18/bento-box-boundaries/

---

**Next Steps**

For more inspiration on saying 'no', see:

Jenny Odell, *How to Do Nothing: Resisting the Attention Economy*. Schwartz Books, 2019.

Melissa Gregg. *Counterproductive: Time Management in the Knowledge Economy*. Duke University Press, 2018.

---

### 4.3.3 Do you need a nap?

Getting some rest should be the easiest thing in the world. It just involves sitting down. And if you have the capacity to sometimes be sitting down at your desk to work on your PhD, you should have the capacity to sometimes be sitting down and taking a break.

Perhaps take it further and take a nap. Maybe go to bed a bit early or get up a bit late. Maybe stretch out on the carpet and zone out, or curl up in the sun with a cup of chamomile tea and do nothing. Maybe slow down a bit before you go to bed, so you can fall asleep.

It's the easiest thing ever. And if you are tired, it's the thing you are longing to do.

If you can't remember when you last felt rested, then you won't be working efficiently or making your best decisions. You aren't doing your physical health, your mental health or your supervisor any favours either.

At a workshop the other day, someone asked about how to get over 'procrastination'—a very common question. Any delay, resistance or pause in the productivity machine is labelled 'procrastination'. But sometimes you are just tired. How can you tell the difference?

One way to tell the difference is by checking in. Ask yourself: are you procrastinating, or do you need a nap? If you are not sure about the answer, you can try this experiment.

Set your timer to 15 minutes. Arrange yourself comfortably on the floor or a sofa and close your eyes. Breathe gently and softly. You may drift off, or you may just have a nice rest for your eyes and brain.

When the alarm goes off, get up, and set your timer for five minutes. Have some water and a snack.

Return to your desk and set the timer for 25 minutes. Look at your document. Do you feel your mind is somehow clearer, do you have more energy, can you string together a few words? Great! Do that! Also, now you know your problem is tiredness and you should plan in some rest and relaxation in the near future. Try a critical distance break!

Naps are great for productivity, so even if you don't really need a nap but you'd like a bit of shut-eye, please go ahead!

Go, get some rest. Take three days, or three hours, or three minutes. Give yourself permission. You'll do better for it.

---

**Notes**

Research suggests having some caffeine before your nap, to time the chemical release of caffeine perfectly. The coffee nap has been studied a number of times, and this article reviews and replicates the findings:

Mitsuo Hayashi, Akiko Masuda, Tadao Hori, 'The Alerting Effects of Caffeine, Bright Light and Face Washing After a Short Daytime Nap', *Clinical Neurophysiology*, 114: 12, 2268–2278. 2003.

For me, the mental impact of caffeine is pretty strong and immediate, so I prefer to have my caffeine when I get up.

A first version of this section was written for *Research Degree Insiders*: https://researchinsiders.blog/2014/05/12/stop-work-more-often/ and https://researchinsiders.blog/2021/11/25/are-you-procrastinating-or-do-you-need-a-nap/

---

**Next Steps**

If you are facing a significant block and it is procrastination, talking to a counsellor or health service at your university can help you find a recharge strategy that is right for your situation.

You don't have to fully nap, you could use a resting version of the 'just thinking' strategy outlined in Section 1.3.6.

---

### 4.3.4 Why researchers should have hobbies

People often think hobbies are for kids or retired people: for people who have holidays that aren't conferences, or weekends that aren't for grant writing. And yet some of the most successful researchers I know, at every level, have hobbies, and often intense and time-consuming ones. They understand that working all the time is not effective. Hobbies are useful for helping you see where, and how, to put up boundaries on your work time, when you might be tempted to answer one more email instead. Plus, having a hobby means you have already decided what you will do when you stop working.

Hobbies are rewarding. They give us a sense of achievement and social connection: whether that's playing a team sport, doing a crossword with your family, or uploading a picture of your sourdough to social media. These things motivate us and make us feel more confident and creative—useful to offset the isolating, unsuccessful or boring aspects of our research. Hobbies remind us that we are more than that last unsuccessful experiment, application, draft or journal submission. We are humans with cool human lives, not just researchers.

Hobbies give us different thinking spaces. Doing something with your hands, exercising, being meditative or creative or excited or playful—these are all great hobby brain-spaces. When I got stuck on my PhD draft, I would go and dig potato trenches in my community garden, or make a loaf of bread. Having these hobbies was really useful for letting ideas simmer or untangle or recombine in different ways. Hobbies are therefore awesome for critical distance breaks.

Hobbies are a form of self-care. Caring for ourselves is not only about health, but also about happiness. Being well in our time, being generous to ourselves about what we enjoy: these are also essential for staying mentally and emotionally well. Hobbies are activities we pursue for pleasure, not out of duty. A hobby is not defined by what you are doing, but why you are doing it. Some people love to have competitive hobbies, others love hobbies with deadlines, and others like hobbies that have detailed rules—and yet other people hate all of these things! None of these aspects makes or breaks a hobby, it's just about what you personally find fun.

Keep your hobbies separate from your research or side hustle. You might enjoy your research, but it's important to keep spaces that are purely for fun or play. If a hobby becomes a job, then you need to go out and find a new hobby. As an adult, finding more work has been easier for me than finding new hobbies, so I guard my hobbies carefully.

Hobbies are great just for themselves. But if you are feeling guilty about taking time for a hobby, or not sure if you should rearrange your week to make time for one, then this section hopefully encourages you to see that it's a great idea.

> **Notes**
>
> A first version of this section was written for *Research Degree Insiders*: https://researchinsiders.blog/2021/03/25/why-busy-researchers-need-hobbies/

### 4.3.5 Cleaning your workspace/cleaning your headspace

If you write in a café, hot desk or on the kitchen table, you will have to tidy your writing space regularly. If you have the luxury of a steady desk space, it can still be supportive to take time to clear it up in times of transition out of writing, before a break. Both your physical and digital workspace can benefit from cleaning up. Archive old papers or files. Make stacks of things you won't need till later. Remove those abandoned coffee cups.

As you are tidying your space, you are thoughtfully engaging with the material. Do I still need this? When will I want it again? How relevant is that to my current project? How can I put it somewhere I will find it again when I need it, in a format that will be useful at that time? All great questions, and equally relevant to washing up and putting away that dirty plate, as it is filing those unread PDFs in your downloads folder.

I like Davis's 'only 5 things' approach to cleaning (2020), and her strategy can be easily adapted to our workspaces. You don't need to be too careful about your tidying up. Broad stacks of things are usually good enough.

1. Discard. Put things into the bin and recycling. Use the bin/trash, delete and unsubscribe functions in your emails and files.
2. Collect any cups, plates and water bottles. Wash them up.
3. Identify any materials that have been borrowed and need to be returned—library books, tools, data, peer-review requests and the like. Put them in one place so you can find them later.
4. What has a place and isn't in it yet? Put PDFs into a folder called 'Upload to EndNote'. Put your pens back into the caddy. Put books on the bookshelf (not necessarily in order, just on the shelf!).
5. What doesn't have a place? Put them in a pile.

You still have three piles of things: stuff that needs to be returned; stuff that doesn't have a home; and stuff that you need to work on when you return to your research. If the stuff that needs to be returned is urgent, deal with it now. Otherwise, make a note of when it will become urgent and set it to one side.

The purpose of this clearing of your workspace and headspace is not to achieve a perfectly clean and tidy desk or computer desktop. It's to make it safe to walk away from the desk while you take a break, to give you space to do other recharge activities, and to make it easy to return to research once your break is over.

As you come back to writing after a break, you'll need to set up your workspace and your headspace. That means cleaning a lot of things off the table in front of you, but it might also mean putting a whole lot of things onto it! Again, it's not about matching some theoretical concept of 'tidy', but rather about preparing your workspace.

As you purposefully clean up or set up your workspace, you are strategizing about what you need and how you will use it. You are also optimizing your workspace and brain-space to be able to move forward effectively with your thesis. Use this as a practical ritual to help you transition back into research after taking a break.

## Notes

KC Davis, *How to Keep House While Drowning: 31 Days of Compassionate Help*. Amazon Digital, 2020.

Rachel Hoffman, *Unf\*ck Your Habitat: You're Better Than Your Mess*. St. Martin's, 2017.

Marie Kondo, *The Life-Changing Magic of Tidying Up: The Japanese Art of Decluttering and Organizing*. Penguin, 2011/2014.

Susan Pinsky, *Organizing Solutions for People with ADHD, 2nd Edition-Revised and Updated: Tips and Tools to Help You Take Charge of Your Life and Get Organized*. Fair Winds, 2012.

A first version of this section was written for *Research Degree Insiders*: https://researchinsiders.blog/2022/02/10/is-it-time-to-de-clutter-your-to-be-read-pile/

> **Next Steps**
>
> Putting random draft files into big folders is the basis of the filing strategy outlined in Section 5.3.4.
>
> These physical space strategies match with digital organization strategies recommended in Tiago Forte, *Building a Second Brain: A Proven Method to Organise Your Digital Life and Unlock Your Creative Potential*. Profile, 2022.
>
> If you need to discard something massive like the whole thesis, you might also want to use a ritual to acknowledge this significant moment (see Section 4.4 and Kondo, 2011/2014).

### 4.3.6 Getting back into writing after a break

People sometimes feel nervous about taking a recharge break because they aren't sure how to get back into the writing at the end of it, especially if it's an extended break like a long holiday, maternity leave, or years in the industry. Here's a strategy I often use to help people get back into academic writing after a long break.

Pat Thomson and I have both used the metaphor of the 'writing starter' to talk about how a daily writing practice can activate your regular writing habit through feeding every one to three days (Thomson 2014, Firth 2016). However, you can have a sourdough starter that you only feed once a week, and you can also rescue a sourdough starter that has not been used for quite a while. It's a process, but it's not a particularly difficult one.

Baking bread, mostly sourdough, was an important part of my wellbeing strategies during my PhD journey and as an early career researcher. I've been a rather less-frequent baker since moving around the corner from some fantastic bakeries, though. Not so long ago, I got my sourdough starter out of the fridge after a month of ignoring it to find it was utterly disgusting. It was grey and wet and smelled of paint thinner. The top was covered in a white yeast and had set like concrete. My starter was in pretty poor shape. There was no way I could give it some flour and bake a loaf.

Fortunately, I've been here before and I know how to revive a starter:

- I scraped off the gunk on top of the starter and threw it away.
- I decanted the starter into a clean container.
- I fed the starter lots of organic rye flour.
- I left the starter out at room temperature.
- As it rose, I fed it again.
- When the smell had returned to a fresh yeasty scent and the starter had doubled, I put it back into the fridge.
- I fed it again for a couple of days. Before the end of the week, I was baking a new loaf.

These steps of reactivating a dormant sourdough starter can also be used to help you think about how to reactivate your writing practice after a pause. If you haven't written for a while, you might sit down at your computer and expect words to come … they might not.

Here are some steps to take in the first few days of getting back into writing, using strategies from across the book but in a slightly different order since you are revising an existing project rather than starting from scratch:

1. Clear out any things that stop you from getting to the writing starter. For example, managers often have to be super responsive to emails and telephone messages, but researchers don't. Turn off notifications for emails and telephone messages while you are writing.
2. Dust off your writing implements and see if they are still fit for purpose. Writing technology changes all the time, and even old favourites can benefit from a refresh.
3. Shifting your brain from caring, resting or emailing to writing can be supported by shifting your place of work. Maybe go onto campus to help you change your brain-space back into writing.
4. Put something into your brain first. For the first session, read an article that activates a reaction from you. Make your first task a review, summary or response to something you have read.
5. Give yourself some time to let the pre-writing get going. Good writing prompts to get back into writing after a break are:

- The reason my research is going to make a difference in the world is …
- No one has done my research before because …
- When I started this project, I wanted to achieve …

6. Feed your brain again. Don't forget to add lunch or a cup of coffee or a drink of water. Do some stretches to get some blood and oxygen back into your brain.

7. Keep your early goals comfortable and achievable. Effective early-stage goals could be: 'make a narrative plan for the chapter', or 'write a summary of this article and explain how it inspires me', or 'write 250 words responding to a writing prompt'.

8. When you reach those goals, stop! You have done a great job. Put it on your done list and give your writing muscles and your brain a break. We're building back up to this slowly, but the writing is going well!

9. Do the same thing again tomorrow. And the day after. You are building a new habit. If you are doing this regularly, you will soon feel comfortable with getting back into the writing.

*Figure 4.2* The loaf I baked after rescuing my sourdough starter

After a few days of this strategy, actually start writing. You don't need to stay in this warm-up and re-entry phase forever. A few days should be plenty for most people to be in a place to 'write for 25 minutes', 'produce 400 first-draft words', and actually start or restart their writing project.

Once you have got back into the writing and produced enough material, remember to give yourself another brief critical distance break before moving on to the next stage of your project, the structural edit.

### Notes

Pat Thompson has written about how blogging keeps her writing ferment going (and her partner uses a different but comparable strategy to reactivate the starter after a holiday). See 'on bread and blogging', 2014, https://patthomson.net/2014/10/27/on-bread-and-blogging

You can find my own blog on 'writing starter' here: https://researchinsiders.blog/2016/08/07/your-writing-starter/

I was convinced I'd learned how to make sourdough this way from Richard Bertinet, *Crust: Bread to Get Your Teeth into*. Kyle Cathie, 2007. And while the pages are covered in smears of dough, his advice is not what I've recommended here, even if it's still a great book for starting to bake bread. Also, never use a starter that has gone mouldy.

A first version of this section was written for *Research Degree Insiders*: https://researchinsiders.blog/2017/04/19/getting-back-into-writing-after-a-break/ and https://researchinsiders.blog/2016/08/07/your-writing-starter/

## Next Steps

After a long break in the middle of your writing process, you'll be drawing resources from across the writing cycle as you get back into the rhythm of writing.

See Section 4.3.5 for other clearing-up options.

Writing technologies change all the time, check out some of them in Section 3.3.2.

Use the practices presented in Section 3. to find your perfect writing set-up, and maybe use the strategies around writing with others from Section 3.3.3. Changing workspaces is suggested in Section 7.2.

Fill your writing brain by jumping back to the generous reading strategies outlined in Section 1.3.5. Use a generative writing prompt like the one in Section 3.1 to warm up for your writing.

Early goals: 'make a narrative plan for the chapter' (see Section 2.4.2), 'write a summary of this article and explain how it inspires me' (see Section 1.3.4), or 'write 250 words responding to a writing prompt' (see Section 3.1).

We discussed done lists in Section 2.3.3 and first-draft words in Section 3.3.1.

## *Reflective practice for recharging: Transition traditions*

Now that you have read this chapter, it's time to reflect on what you want to take forward and put into practice.

It often takes us a while to get into, or out of, a state of recharging. Rituals can help you transition from one space to another. These can be very mundane or quite elaborate. Reflect on the following questions:

- As you are about to finish work, what are your transition rituals to mark the end of the day? Do you make a done list, close a door, commute?
- As you are about to start work, how do you set an intention for the time coming up? Do you state your goal or visualize your success? Perhaps you have a writing playlist, a special writing coffee cup, a writing candle, or a lucky pen.

If you don't currently have a ritual, reflect on what you might like to include in your ritual.

You might use reflection tools like journaling, talking to a colleague, or mindfulness activities (discussed in Chapters 1–3 and Section 4.2).

### Next Steps

For exploring organizational and research rituals, see:

Casper Ter Kuile, *The Power of Ritual: Turning Everyday Activities into Soulful Practices*. HarperCollins Publishers, 2020.

Marie Kondo, *The Life-Changing Magic of Tidying Up: The Japanese Art of Decluttering and Organizing*. Penguin, 2011/2014.

*Your PhD Survival Guide* has some specific rituals for the end of your PhD that may also be helpful, see pp. 193–194.

# Editing
## Getting your thesis into shape

Writing is for authors, editing is for readers. Editing requires us to take a big-picture view, be critical about our own writing, and really think about the reader. This is the opposite of the writing stage: when we need to focus on getting each word down, where it's fine if the writing is terrible or rough, and where we are thinking about what we are trying to say. Now it's time to focus on how others will read our work.

Editing is the generous act of giving your writing away to readers. That generosity requires us to think deeply about the other person and work to meet their needs. You will also have your own feelings about the process and that is valid too!

Structural editing is about making sure your draft contains the right information in a logical order. It gives you the big picture of what your writing is doing, the level of feedback that an editor will give you when you submit work for publication. Editing functions at the chapter, section and paragraph levels of writing. Questions of scope, of argument, and of producing a cohesive contribution are answered in the editing phase.

Editing is when we return to our overall plan. Perhaps we see that the written document does not match the plan, and we need to edit our draft so it is closer to our plan. Or perhaps we see that our plan is no longer the most accurate map for explaining our research, and we need to use the editing stage to rewrite our plan so it is useful for progressing our draft.

Do not merge or reverse the editing and polishing stages. You can spend hours on formatting, word choice, and references, only to realize that a paragraph or a whole section is extraneous to the current project and needs to be cut. Be kind to yourself and your research deadlines by restructuring at the macro-level (whole of thesis or chapter) and the meso-level (paragraphs and sections) first.

DOI: 10.4324/9781003307945-6

## 5.1 A mindfulness practice for editing: Imagining your ideal reader

Who are you writing for? In the first place, you are writing for yourself. You will read and edit. Then your supervisors will read and edit. Eventually your examiners will read and make revision suggestions. If you try to write so that 'everyone' can read it, you will end up not writing for 'anyone'. Instead, it's best to imagine one or two ideal readers and write just for them, to make something that reads better for everyone.

Let's step into the mind of our ideal reader, using our imagination. You want to write in a way that addresses your reader's questions without spending too long rehashing what they already know, and clearly explain anything they don't know yet. In other words, you are using 'theory of mind'. Frith and Frith (2005) explain:

> We naturally explain people's behavior on the basis of their minds: their knowledge, their beliefs and their desires, and we know that when there is a conflict between belief and reality it is the persons' belief, not the reality that will determine their behavior. Explaining behavior in this way is called 'having a theory of mind' or 'having an intentional stance'.

If you have ever worked in communications, you might know about 'personas', representations of example audience members. These are semi-fictional, you make up a name, identity and back story, but base it on what you know about your target audience. I created five personas for my previous book, *Your PhD Survival Guide*, and I continue to use them to help me edit this book in a way that will meet the needs of a range of readers from around the world, studying different degrees and with different life experiences.

Maybe your ideal reader is a specific person, like a world-famous scholar you admire, or a colleague in your department. In that case, start out by identifying what you know about their academic interests: use their publications and conference presentations to work out what they think is important, how they understand the world, what their pet peeves are. They may even have a blog or social media account where they tell you more.

Maybe your ideal reader belongs to a specific group—urban geographers who are interested in climate change policy; viral disease researchers who are also using nanoparticles; education researchers who work on intercultural early childhood learning. Research across a range of real people in your group and then create a fictional composite exemplar who represents that group.

Let's build a persona:

1.  Find a picture of your ideal reader (either a real headshot or a generic stock photo from the internet). Put it on a page or PowerPoint slide.
2.  Give your reader a name, a place of work, a discipline and research interest, a level of seniority.
3.  What does your reader want to achieve? What are their biggest research goals?
4.  What are their pain points? What do they find difficult, confusing or unpleasant that your research might solve?
5.  What is your take-home message for them? Define what is new, interesting or useful about your work for this reader.
6.  Put your persona up on a noticeboard or in your notebook. Before you start editing, remind yourself who you are writing for and what they want out of your thesis.

Use this ideal reader persona to inspire you, to help you make good editorial choices, and to stay connected to the community of scholars who can't wait to read your work!

## Options

If you are writing an interdisciplinary thesis, make sure you make at least two personas, one for each discipline.

Perhaps your ideal reader is beyond the academy. It's likely that they won't read about your research in its thesis form, but instead in a report, a flyer, a newspaper article or a video explainer. When you are rewriting your research, it can help to clearly imagine some new personas, and then write for them.

## Notes

Chris Frith and Uta Frith, 'Theory of mind', *Current Biology*, 15:17, R644–R645. 2005.

## 5.2 A physical wellbeing practice for editing: Three breathing exercises before you start editing

Breathing is amazing. Your body can breathe perfectly well on its own, but the lungs are also the only organ over which we have total, immediate, mind control. You can decide to hold your breath, or to breathe fast or slow, and your lungs will just do it! Decide to breathe deeply using your belly, or to breathe shallowly just in your upper chest, and your lungs will respond.

The connection works the other way too. Your brain checks in on your breathing to find out how things are going in the body, including to work out if it should help out by pumping out stress or calm reactions. So choosing your breath can help you influence your emotions. You can add to the messages you are sending your brain by explicitly thinking a useful positive phrase, like 'I can take this slow if I need to, but I can definitely make progress today', or 'deadlines coming, let's get a move on'.

Which feelings will help you be in the best mindset to edit today? Maybe you would like to be calmer, or get fired up, or to be balanced. Pick the relevant breathing exercise for you today. For each of the exercises, I'll tell you why you'd use it, why it works and how to do it, I'll also suggest a little affirmation that you can try out.

**A calming breath for when writing stresses you out in a bad way**: If you sit down to write and feel your 'flight' or 'freeze' stress reaction activate because you want to run away from the scary writing, then that will get in the way of the thing you want to do, which is stick at the desk and write some words.

If you listen to someone breathing in their sleep, you might notice they breathe through their nose for a diaphragmatic inhale of about a count of three, they pause for a count of one or two, and then they exhale through their nose for a longer count of five or more. Breathing this way tells your brain it's probably safe enough for a mini-nap, so you turn off the flight or fright reaction and get into a more 'rest and digest' state where you can sit at a desk and digest your ideas into writing.

How to do it:

1. Sit at your desk.
2. Set a timer for two minutes, select a soothing notification sound at the end.

3. Breathe in through your nose, counting 1, 2, 3.
4. Pause with filled lungs for 1, 2.
5. Breathe out through your nose for 1, 2, 3, 4, 5 or even more.
6. Adjust so it feels comfortable to you, like you are in a light sleep.
7. Repeat until the timer goes off.
8. Return to your habitual, normal breath.

Repeat this as many times as you need to before each 'scary' action: sitting at your desk, opening the document, reading the feedback and so on.

Remind yourself: 'I am in charge of this, even if it's not pleasant. I can do this. I can get this done!'

**An energizing breath for firing up your writing:** I love to write angry. When I'm fired up and passionate, I write fast and I enjoy the writing process, a lot of my blogging comes from rage writing. The other part of the 'flight and freeze' response is the 'fight' instinct. If you find feeling like fighting gets you excited about writing, then a calming breath isn't going to help you, you'll need something to fire you up instead.

If you listen to someone breathing after challenging exercise or when they are excited, you might notice they use a deep short inhale of about three, a short sharp exhale of one or two, with perhaps a mini-pause before they inhale again. If they use their diaphragm and can breathe through their nose, they won't go over into being out of breath, though. This breathing tells your brain that there's something to work against, that it's time to get ready to rumble, that it's exciting or that there's some serious exertion going on here. Build up some heat and then let that pour out of your fingers.

How to do it:

1. Sit at your desk.
2. Set a timer for two minutes, select an action notification sound at the end.
3. Breathe in through your nose, counting 1, 2 (3).
4. Breathe out fast through your nose for 1, 2.
5. Pause with emptied lungs for 1.
6. Adjust so you can sustain the pattern without becoming breathless.
7. Repeat until the timer goes off.
8. Return to your habitual, normal breath.

Remind yourself: 'This needs doing, and I am just the person to get it done. Watch out, world!'

**An equal breath for balanced thinking:** Maybe this is the day for careful, balanced thought. Maybe this work is boring, but you do need to focus. You need to be judicious, even-handed, accurate and steady, and you want a breath that helps you with that.

This exercise is all about the counting. It's just complicated enough that you can't multitask. You have to focus on this one thing. The equal breathing means your brain should settle into a state that's not too sleepy and not too fired up but just-Goldilocks-right for the task.

How to do it:

1. Sit at your desk.
2. Set a timer for two minutes, select a neutral notification at the end.
3. Breathe in through your nose, counting 1, 2, 3.
4. Pause with filled lungs for 1, 2, 3.
5. Breathe out through your nose for 1, 2, 3.
6. Pause with emptied lungs for 1, 2, 3.
7. Repeat for one minute, then extend each count to 1, 2, 3, 4.
8. Repeat until the timer goes off.
9. Return to your habitual, normal breath.

Remind yourself: 'I will proceed at a steady pace through this task, ticking things off.'

And there you have it. Three kinds of breathing exercises to get you in the mood for writing. I hope that they help you, and that you find ways to tweak them so they work even better for you!

---

### Options

If the suggested breathing is distracting or uncomfortable, breathe however works best for you. Use the two minutes, the counting, the notification sound, and the reminder phrases to get you into the mindset.

Rewrite any of the affirmations so they address your individual mindset and situation.

**Notes**

For more extensive detail on breathing techniques, see:

Patrick McKeown, *The Oxygen Advantage: The Simple, Scientifically Proven Breathing Technique that Will Revolutionise Your Health and Fitness.* Little, Brown, 2015.

James Nestor, *Breath: The New Science of a Lost Art.* Penguin, 2020.

A first version of this section was written for *Research Degree Insiders*: https://researchinsiders.blog/2021/02/04/3-breathing-exercises-before-you-start-writing/

## 5.3 How to edit: Different strategies

Before you start to edit, it's helpful to go back to the plans you made for your writing: what did you decide was essential to cover in the dialogical, narrative or visual planning techniques you used? What was the logical progression you expected to take? What was in and out of scope? How important were the different sections?

Now as you come to structurally edit your work, you can assess whether the plan was accurate. Reflect on the following:

- What didn't happen? Is that something that you need to fix? Or did the process of writing up your draft uncover new pathways that were more important or accurate?
- Did the logical sequence from your plan work out in your draft? If not, what is the new logical sequence, and does it work better?
- Did the proportions of each section match how important they are? You should spend most words on the most important information. Do you need to adjust your sections, or have new priorities emerged?
- Is everything in the draft relevant to the argument? If not, do you need to cut material or update your argument?
- What is out of order? Does everything line up to prove your contention, to prove your original contribution to knowledge?
- What is missing? Is there anything essential in your research that you didn't put into the draft?

The technical aspects of the editing stage are well covered in the many style guides and academic writing books. This section first focuses on how we can conceptualize and think through editing, and then offers some practical insider tips for putting these into practice, so you can write well and do good through your writing.

---

**Next Steps**

Reviewing the plans you made in Chapter 2 can be helpful here.

See Sections 5.3.3 and 8.3.2 for more lists of useful editing books or check out *How to Fix Your Academic Writing Trouble*, Chapters 6 and 7, and *Your PhD Survival Guide*, Chapter 10 for more practical editing advice.

---

### 5.3.1 Be your own best critic

In literary studies, 'critique' and 'critical thinking' are the highest forms of rigour, and they are positive terms. If I'm talking to someone in everyday conversation, and they say, 'I've got some criticisms of you', I expect them to be pretty scathing about lots of things that are wrong with me. When I sit down to read literary criticism, however, I expect to hear a lot about what is good about the work.

At the same time, 'is it any good?' is often the least interesting or important part of literary criticism. My research field is cultural studies/cultural history, so some of my favourite criticism starts with 'this isn't great art, but it's interesting' or 'who cares if it's good or not, lots of people love it, let's look at why' or 'this art is good, but it's also extremely problematic, let's unpack that'. So critical questions can be more about how your work sits within wider contexts than just 'how can this work be better?'

If you are 'your own worst critic', you could explore transforming into your own 'best critic': not by turning your 'inner critic' into an 'inner cheerleader', but by training your inner critic to be good at their job.

So what is a good critic? A good critic can identify where writing is strong or weak, where things are coherent and internally logical, and where things don't fully make sense. A good critic not only identifies such issues, but also has a strong sense of how to make the writing better. How they identify issues in your writing helps you make productive changes.

A good critic evaluates your work compared to your peers and a model of 'good writing'. A good critic is widely read in the genre you are working in, and has a deep understanding of what your sort of writing typically looks like, along with a historically informed understanding of what is 'traditional' and what is 'innovative' in your field. A good critic can therefore evaluate where you could learn from others, and where you stand out compared to your peers. Such a reader will also see connections between your work and the work of others, perhaps seeing influences that are not obvious, or places where your writing is in conversation with other wider debates. That helps you to read effectively across a range of sources, and to improve your citations.

What's more, a good critic recognizes development across your body of work. A good critic is interested not only in what you are doing well, or not so well, right now, but they can also see how far you have developed since your early days as a writer. They can see what you are doing in the current work that is new, exciting or more mature. They may identify some strengths in your earlier writing that have been lost, that you might want to recapture. They can also see the consistent threads through your whole body of work: recurrent themes, approaches, or a sustained writerly voice.

A good critic sees depths others may have missed, and uncovers latent meanings. A good critic reads your work looking for deep understanding, but also for ambiguities and tensions in your writing. Sometimes, these deeper meanings are something you intended, and it's great that other readers perceive and appreciate them. Sometimes, those further meanings are unintentional, and they muddy the purpose of your writing. Catching those unclear meanings early gives you a chance to rewrite your text for greater clarity.

The job of a critic goes beyond merely responding to your writing, however. Literary criticism produces new works that extend your ideas, apply them in new contexts or explain their ongoing relevance. A good critic will help you to see where your research can go next, and how it can be developed into future writing projects, future collaborations, or be applied in future contexts.

Finally, a good critic introduces your work to new readers. A good critic helps your writing heroes find your work, and find it useful. Other readers who discover you are probably scholars you want to be reading in turn, so this aspect of a critic's job will help you find new heroes too.

Just imagine how awesome it would be to have a good inner critic, helping you write well, understanding your writing process, and getting your writing into the hands of readers who want to read it. Give your inner critic some professional development so they become good at their job!

**Notes**

The definition of criticism described here is discussed by scholars, including T. S. Eliot, *The Use of Poetry and the Use of Criticism: Studies in the Relation of Criticism to Poetry in England*. Faber, 1933; Northrop Frye, *Anatomy of Criticism*. Princeton, 1957; and Gayatri Chakravorty Spivak, *In Other Worlds: Essays in Cultural Politics*. Taylor & Francis, 2012.

On ambiguities, see William Empson, *Seven Types of Ambiguity*. New Directions, 1966.

A first version of this section was written for *Research Degree Insiders*: https://researchinsiders.blog/2019/07/18/be-your-own-best-critic/

**Next Steps**

Some literary criticism that I have enjoyed includes works by Virginia Woolf, Edward Said, Toni Morrison and Walter Benjamin.

Many significant social theorists are also literary critics, so you might use your methodology to find relevant criticism.

### 5.3.2 How to create a logical structure

Western logical structures, which developed from the ancient Greeks and were then built on by Church Fathers and Enlightenment philosophers, tend to be what we mean when we say we want your argument to 'progress logically' (Aristotle, 350 BCE; Aquinas, 1485; Kant, 1781). Wellbeing is often placed in opposition to rigorous, logical, excellent academic achievement. But as Foucault reminds us in the *Care of the Self*, drawing on Plato, Seneca and Marcus Aurelius, Western logics are also based on a rigorous practice of the care or 'cultivation of the self' (pp. 48–49). Furthermore, as bell hooks reminds us, such logics can be 'liberatory' or 'healing' if used for good (2014, p. 61).

Understanding Western logical norms means you can finally crack the code of why your supervisor keeps writing 'I'm not sure this is a logical progression' on your manuscript. Of course, there are other forms of logic, both forms that are equally ancient and newer forms that challenge this pattern. So if you are doing quantum physics, postmodern philosophy, or Indigenous story work, it can be helpful to understand what readers are expecting, to establish that you are doing something different, and to explain why it's right for your project.

Perhaps the easiest and best-known form of logical progression is the syllogism. If you don't already know about syllogisms, they are a very simple kind of logical structure to work out what claims you are making, what deductions you are making from those claims, and where it might be going wrong.

The ancient Greek philosopher and father of the syllogism, Aristotle, uses the formula:

*All men are mortal.*
*Socrates is a man.*
*Therefore, Socrates is mortal.*

This is a very neat logical argument. Yay!

The syllogism is a good way to run through a logical checklist. Every time we ask if something is logical, we are asking questions like:

- What are you assuming? Is it correct?
- What are the facts? Do you fully understand them?
- What is the order in which things occur?
- Is there causation, correlation or just coincidence?
- What conclusions can we draw from our argument?

As you have probably noticed when trying to construct your arguments for your thesis, there are lots of ways you could go wrong with your logical progression. The main ways you could go wrong with your logical progressions are:

- You assume things are true when they are not true.
- You assume things are true for everything and they are only true for a specific set of those things.
- Or you leave out an assumption that means you have a serious logical gap.

119

A tool like the syllogism can help you identify what they are, and then fix them. It can be easier to understand how this works with some examples.

1.  If you assume things are true when they are not true, your logical fallacy (mistake) might be something like the version set out in Table 5.1.
2.  If you assume things are true for everything and they are only true for a specific set of those things, your logical fallacy might be something like Table 5.2.
3.  If you leave out an assumption (or step), which means you have a serious logical gap, your logical fallacy might be like Table 5.3.

The bigger and more complex your argument, not only do you need to put in more steps, but you also introduce more steps that could be wrong, or not quite right, or be missing.

*Table 5.1* Logical fallacy: Wrong assumptions

| Claim | Comments |
| --- | --- |
| Aristotle died in 322 BCE. | *(BCE = before the common era.)* *This is a historical fact.* |
| The Classical period in Ancient Greece ended in 323 BCE. | *This is widely accepted to be a valid definition of the Classical period.* |
| **Therefore** the death of Aristotle led to the end of the Classical Period. | **False**. *Years BCE go backwards, so Aristotle's death happened after the end of the Classical era.* |

*Table 5.2* Logical fallacy: Over-generalization

| Claim | Comments |
| --- | --- |
| All mammals have tails. | *Only some mammals have tails, although all have vestiges of tails.* |
| Humans are mammals. | *This is a fact.* |
| **Therefore**, humans have tails. | **False**. *Only some mammals have tails. Humans are among the mammals that do not have tails.* |

Table 5.3 Logical fallacy: Missing a step in the argument

| Claim | Comments |
|---|---|
| Aristotle died in 322 BCE. | *As before, this is a historical fact.* |
| The Classical period in Ancient Greece ended in 323 BCE. | *Again, this is widely accepted to be a valid definition of the Classical period.* |
| — | *However, the Classical period ends in 323 BCE at the death of Alexander the Great. Aristotle was Alexander the Great's tutor. Aristotle fled Athens after the new rulers took power. Nonetheless, he is believed to have died of natural causes.* |
| **Therefore**, the death of Aristotle was caused by the end of the Classical Period. | **False**. *While this fixes the chronology problem of the first syllogism, with the extra information included, the argument is factually incorrect.* |

If you have the right tool for logically working through it, you can work through it methodically and solve the issues. Try mapping out sections where there are problems with the logic using tables like those shown earlier.

Logical progressions like this represent truth claims. Good writing is not only orderly, but honest. This is why something as technical as organizing your argument also has implications for doing good. We should interrogate our logical structures to ensure we are not using them as weapons to destroy or put down other people, but rather to use 'theory as liberatory practice' to empower and enlighten (hooks 2014, p. 59).

## Notes

Aristotle, Categories. *On Interpretation. Prior Analytics*, translated by HP Cooke and Hugh Tredennick. Loeb Classical Library 325. Harvard University Press, 1938. See especially 'Prior Analytics' on συλλογισμὸν (syllogisms), I.2, 24b18–20.

Immanuel Kant, *Critique of Pure Reason*, translated and edited by Paul Guyer and Allen W Wood, Cambridge University Press, 1781/1787/1998. See A50/B74, pp. 193 following.

Thomas Aquinas, *Opera Omnia: Ut sunt in Indice Thomistico Additis 61 Scriptis ex Aliis Medii Aevi Auctoribus*, edited Roberto Busa. Frommann-Holzboog, 1980. See particularly the 'Five Ways of Deduction', *Summa Theologiae*, Volume 2, Part 1, Question 2, Articles 1–3, pp. 187–188.

Michel Foucault, *History of Sexuality, Care of the Self, Volume 3, Cultivation of the Self*, translated by Robert Hurley. Penguin, 1984/2020.

Marcus Aurelius, *Meditations in Marcus Aurelius*, edited and translated by CR Haines. Loeb Classical Library 58. Harvard University Press, 1916.

bell hooks, *Teaching to Transgress*. Taylor & Francis, 2014. We come back to this idea in more detail in Section 7.3.4

Jason De Santolo, Jenny Bol Jun Lee-Morgan, Jo-ann Archibald, and Q'um Q'um Xiiem, editors, *Decolonizing Research: Indigenous Storywork as Methodology*. Bloomsbury, 2019.

A first version of this section was written for *Research Degree Insiders*: https://researchinsiders.blog/2020/01/16/what-is-a-logical-progression-and-how-do-i-make-one/

## Next Steps

Use your reader personas developed in Section 5.1 to work out what kinds of logics your examiners might expect. How do you explain your logical progressions to them?

We also explore ways that these logical philosophical traditions can be used to support our wellbeing in journaling (see Section 1.37) and in rewriting (see Section 7.3.4).

### 5.3.3 Editing paragraphs to be steps in your argument

A paragraph is a step in an argument. Like a good step in a staircase, it should be clearly delineated and take you in smooth and even stages towards your goal. Each step should be big enough for your foot to securely stand on it, but not so big you need to walk between risers. It should have enough of a lift for you to make progress but not be so large that you need to struggle or jump to get from stage to stage. The whole staircase should be aligned, and well-lit so you can see your way forward.

Not every stair in the whole journey needs to be exactly the same, though. You might have stairs that need to go around corners, or use different materials. With very long or complex staircases, you may not be able to see all the way to your destination from the first step, but you should be able to see at least the first flight. For structural editing, you must check that each step is part of a larger set of stairs, the flight.

Paragraphs are parts of sections. And the sections make up your chapter, and the chapters make up your thesis. A section might be delineated by numbering or a header, or just by an extra topic sentence added to the first paragraph. Sometimes sections are very distinct, for example as you move from context to methods, or from reporting your data to analysing it. Sometimes, the sections will be very similar in theme, content and structure, for example if you are using them to show development over time, or comparing results across locations.

So there is a lot of freedom in how you make a section relate to other sections. Sometimes, a single flight of stairs will take you from one floor to the next, but often, you will need to turn on a half-landing or navigate a mezzanine. These 'flat' spaces are also essential: they allow you to get more height out of a staircase efficiently with a smaller footprint, and allow a reader to pause and survey the next flight more comfortably.

The flat spaces also allow for transitions between sizes or types of stairs. In my Victorian-era house, the stairs from the front hall up to the half-landing are wide and gracious. The less-public stairs from the landing to the first floor are much narrower and less grand, which gives us more useable space in the upstairs rooms. Within each flight, the stairs are consistent and within a section the writing should be consistent in purpose, tone and structure. But you can adjust paragraphs as you move from one section to another.

You should be able to see the whole step before you proceed. In writing paragraphs, this means you need a topic sentence: an overview that tells you what's in the paragraph, how it relates to the overall argument, and how it makes progress towards your final goal. This will usually be possible to work out from the context, but no one likes to have to put their foot on a step they can't quite see clearly. So always include a topic sentence.

A step should have solidity. A step that is not robust, well-supported by evidence or theory, or coherent with the rest of the argument, will feel loose and unsafe. Anchor your paragraph with information from your methodology, theory or data.

A step should make progress towards your goal. How does this step advance your argument? If it doesn't advance your argument, is it necessary? Still, progress towards your goal will be incremental, step-by-step. If you cram too much into a single paragraph, the reader has to jump too far from one step to the next.

A step should be smoothly continuous with the steps before and after. Generally your paragraphs should be about the same length. Consistency leads to a smoother reading experience. Uneven steps mean you are more likely to trip or stumble. If your reader is skimming, rather than plodding, through the text, these safety strategies are even more important. A skim reader is more likely to stumble or get lost if your paragraphs are mismatched or incomplete.

If there is a step missing, that is terrifying for the reader. If your reader ever has to make a dizzying jump across a gap in your argument, they may decide it's safer to back out—not something you want an examiner or reviewer to consider. Including a linking sentence helps bridge any gaps.

For a continuous body paragraph, though, there is often no need to wrap up the paragraph or link forward to the next paragraph. Simply by placing another small step immediately after this one, you create a sense of continuity and forward motion. If you end-stop your paragraphs too much, you interrupt the flow of stepping through the section as a whole. Unless there's a reason to take a pause mid-staircase, just let me keep on moving. There's a lot of thesis left to read before my deadline. However, a section introduction should definitely link forward, and a conclusion should absolutely finish conclusively.

It should be obvious when you move from steps to landings. Signal clearly when we need to turn a corner, or when the steps have finished and we have arrived at the next floor. Always signpost when you are changing direction or coming to a stop.

Use other safety rails to keep the reader on track and help them regain their footing if they need it. PhD thesis staircases are technical, very long and only accessed by experts. Imagine your stairs as the practical metal kind that snake up a high-rise scaffold or zigzag down the retaining wall of a reservoir. Extra safety features will become more important the longer your text is. Give your reader more security through consistent terminology, formatting and numbering, plus clear and descriptive section headings.

Make each step solid, economical and consistent. There's no need to waste a lot of words fancying up your paragraphs. Keep it lean and based on your evidence. If you have extra words in your budget, use them to further secure your theoretical foundations, connect your work more firmly to your argument, or clarify what is in scope for the project. Solid and well-designed paragraphs help your reader feel safe and confident as they work through your original, challenging and extensive contribution to knowledge.

**Notes**

For more technical advice on signposting, see *Your PhD Survival Guide*, pp. 155–156.

A first version of this section was written for *Research Degree Insiders*: https://researchinsiders.blog/2021/08/19/how-to-write-a-paragraph/

**Next Steps**

Go back to walking through your plan (see Section 2.2). How does it feel to walk through your draft?

There are some great resources for editing your paragraphs or developing your argument including, see:

Patrick Dunleavy, *Authoring a PhD: How to Plan, Draft, Write and Finish a Doctoral Thesis or Dissertation*. Palgrave Macmillan, 2017.

Pat Thomson and Barbara Kamler. *Helping Doctoral Students Write: Pedagogies for Supervision*. Taylor & Francis, 2014.

Rachael Cayley, *Explorations of Style blog*: https://explorationsofstyle.com

William T FitzGerald, Joseph Bizup, Joseph M Williams, Wayne C Booth, and Gregory G Colomb, *The Craft of Research*, 4th Edition. University of Chicago Press, 2016.

*How to Fix your Academic Writing Trouble*, Section 3.3, pp. 44–46.

### 5.3.4 Why your filing system matters for structural editing

Well-structured filing systems help create well-structured drafts. In a major writing project like a thesis, multiple chapters need to be brought together. In building towards each completed chapter, you will have multiple documents: fragments of drafts, first drafts, edited drafts, drafts with feedback. If you are writing a co-authored article, then the complexity increases again.

In my last four books, each co-author contributed different sections, so each chapter was a mess of multiple files with multiple authors writing to slightly different timelines. We then read each other's work and gave feed-back. The original author then edited their own section. We then put all the sections together into chapters and started editing the work as a whole. Obviously we needed to use a cloud-based collaborative platform to store and share all of these files. But more importantly, we needed a consistent filing system that made it easy to find the bits and put them together in a meaningful order.

Because academic texts tend to have a consistent structure, you can build a standard filing system that, with minor tweaks, can be used across any thesis- or book-length project. Start with a folder called 'Submission Regulations'. Find all the documents that are required for handing the work in: the massive PDF of formatting guidelines for the PhD (yes there will be one!), the PhD examinations policy, library repository instructions, the copy-editing questionnaire. Save any website or email with relevant infor-mation in it as a document and add it to your folder. Your future self will thank you. Do not skip this step. It's a top tip.

Next, create a folder for each chapter. Each time you do substantial work on your manuscript, you should save the document as a new file. For most people, that means a file for each day you work on the document. Save all of these versions of the draft in the same folder. You might also add your reading, notes and plans to this folder, perhaps in a sub-folder, but keep it all in one place.

Make a folder for past drafts. You should keep copies of old files, as you sometimes make a change that you want to revert. Also, if something crashes and your current draft is corrupted beyond repair, you can pull up the last draft and recover your document with very little work lost. But most days you don't need the old drafts, and it's unhelpful to have them cluttering up your main workspace. It's too easy to waste a day working on the wrong file, so put it somewhere you won't click on it by accident.

Next, decide on a helpful file naming system that helps you sort your files, see what's missing, and see what *is* there. And that means Numbering Your Files. If you publish a book, you typically submit chapters as separate num-bered files to the publisher, so this is an industry norm. You can use punctu-ation like ! for front matter, and start your numbering at 0 for the Intro if you want to keep 1 for Chapter 1.

You can include lots of information in a file name these days, so do! Include who has worked on the file as well, so you can see which files your supervisors have read, and where you have actioned their feedback. Use a date format that is easily sortable, like year-month-day.

For example:

! Front Matter
0.1 Introduction 20-06-25 KEF
0.2 Introduction 20-05-11 JAL
0.2 Introduction 20-05-11 JAL edits KEF
0.2 Introduction 20-05-30 JAL edited
1.1 Chapter 1 20-03-15 KEF

Reading these file names, you can see that the second section of the Introduction has gone through a first draft, an edit, and a new draft. Easily sort the list by file name to find the most recent version, and move the older versions to the past drafts folder.

These naming conventions also make it easier to project manage a co-authored project, to see who has written their sections and who hasn't, or to see which sections haven't been edited yet. A PhD with publications is likely to have multiple articles in various stages of peer review, and so a clear file-naming system will help you track progress.

Obviously, it would have been fantastic if you had created a clear filing system at the beginning of the project, but most people just dump everything in a PhD folder for a while, and then only come to this need for structuring the folders as the project starts to get overwhelmingly big and messy. The editing stage is when we decide to tidy everything up and put it in order. The beauty of digital file storage, as with digital text files, is that it is so easy to improve them later.

You can glance over the file list and see if the overall structure makes sense. If you need to reorder your chapters, it's pretty easy to renumber your files, but do leave a note about the old numbering in the file name or document, so you can find the old drafts (e.g. '1 Chapter 1 used to be chapter 7 20-04-12.docx') and ensure you catch any continuity issues in your final rewrites.

Once you have stored all of these documents in a clear and structured way, it's time to stitch all these bits together and make it a coherent whole. Using a strategic filing system like this is a way to clean and clear your work-space and your headspace, and to lay out for your future self the writing materials you will need, ready for when you need them.

**Notes**

There is no need for this filing system to be too fine-grained. In fact, as Whittaker et al. (2011) found, search functions will help you find any specific document you are searching for. Folders are more about clearing and defining workspaces than establishing retrieval systems. Steve Whittaker, Tara Matthews, Julian Cerruti, Hernan Badenes and John Tang, 'Am I Wasting My Time Organizing Email? A Study of Email Refinding', in *Proceedings of the SIGCHI Conference on Human Factors in Computing Systems*, 3449–3458, 2011.

A first version of this section was written for *Research Degree Insiders*: https://researchinsiders.blog/2020/07/16/what-matters-isnt-your-writing-software/

**Next Steps**

If everything is overwhelming and messy, not just your filing system, it might be time to head back to Section 4.3.5 and give your whole workspace (digital or physical) a clear-up edit.

If your drafts and fragments are in a range of different formats and software packages (as recommended in Section 3.3.2), take some time to go through and export them all into files that can be collected into these folders.

### 5.3.5 Putting the whole draft together

It's time to put the whole thing together. Gather together all the scraps and pieces of your chapter, or indeed your whole thesis, and get them into order in your draft. As with getting a first draft done, the platform is less important here than understanding the principles. You might do this work on screen, on paper, with high-level outlines, or working directly in the text.

There are three essentials that will make a critical difference to your edits:

1. clear headings
2. a way to capture the history of the section
3. a way to move between the paragraph details and the full picture.

Make the headings really clear by using a distinct format. Most word-processing software has official heading styles, and using them helps you create a table of contents. This automatically creates an outline to see how the sections relate to one another. Double-check that you haven't left anything major out and see if your logical order is logical.

Using numbering is helpful. For early drafts, you can go wildly granular in numbering your headings if you want to. And make the headings super descriptive. Of course, in the final 'polish' stage, you will reformat your headings into the approved style guide format. But for now, we are focused on the structural edit. Your working subheadings should help you write and edit your thesis. Don't just say 'Methods': describe what is actually in the section. Use more than one sentence if you need to. Talk about what goes there, the themes, any instructions for your future self. This is also the place to make notes for your future self:

> 1.1.i.a.1 Introduction, REWRITE THIS LAST, 300 words, see the Conclusion for the argument (1.7.iii.b.4)

Tracking changes can only do so much, especially if you ever make edits on paper print-outs or across multiple users. Tracking all those changes also start to make your drafts crash if you have too many of them. So you will periodically need to move to a new 'clean' document. If you edit with a pen on paper, then you can see the scribbles in the current draft, but it can be hard to work out what happened two or three drafts ago.

Therefore, include information about major revision histories in your drafts. I am a fan of using the header or footer of a document to include the file name, draft number, date, page number, the history of who has written or edited it. Then it's on every page, even if you print it out and reorder it. Add a comment in the margin or a line under your headings to help you to trace your way back. Name your files, chapters and sections with their full revision history.

For a recent book, we decided to totally reorder the chapters right before the final submission. We'd already put in a lot of cross-references, so we needed to go through and fix every single one. All of them were now wrong. I would never have managed it if I hadn't renamed each of the headings '6.2 USED TO BE 7.2 How to be more concise'. These ugly but useful headings were a gift, and I was so grateful for them.

In the structural editing stage, you need to jump from the big picture to the paragraph, so you can write meaningful topic sentences and other sign-posting sentences. Ideally, you want to be able to view both your outline and your text simultaneously as you work on the document. Check that the prose flows in a logical way to match the big-picture map of your outline. A side point should not take up twice as much space as the main argument, even if it is fascinating. Gauge that the amount of writing in a section is proportional to its importance.

The closer to the end of the writing project you are, the more important these features become. I can sometimes get away with being sloppy across the first chapter, because I can hold most of it in my head, and I've worked on the content recently enough to remember what I changed and why. But at the end of a project, with tens of thousands of words written over many years, a well-documented structure becomes essential.

Writing your headings in this way is generous to your future self. You are allowed to forget things, to need to change things, or to accept feedback. There is space for mess and exploration and play. You don't have to get it right the first time. In fact, academic writing always involves compromises. A section that seems strangely messy or empty or you can't remember why it's in such a weird order will be baffling to your future self, but if you have descriptive headings that explain their complex history and help you see the big picture, then you can make more informed decisions about your next steps.

Again, you might not have started structuring your drafts this way, and that's not a problem. You can reverse engineer this neatness to achieve order and calm, as well as a well-edited PhD thesis.

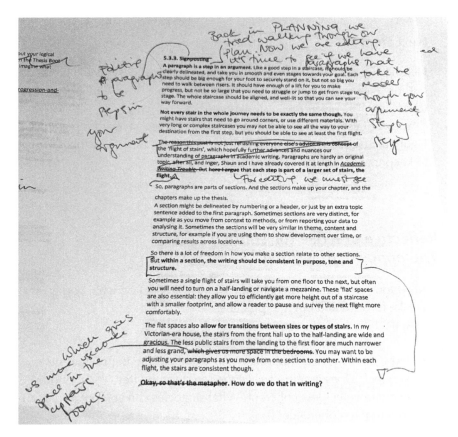

*Figure 5.1* My structural edits for Section 5.3.3

## Notes

A first version of this section was written for *Research Degree Insiders*: https://researchinsiders.blog/2020/07/16/what-matters-isnt-your-writing-software/

**Next Steps**

Getting the big picture might also involve a process like 'reverse outlining' the whole thesis. For more detail, see *Your PhD Survival Guide*, pp. 153–155.

You can also see a screenshot of my computer navigation pane in Figure 6.1 (section 6.3.1), which illustrates the outline view that I use to keep track of the overall structure of my drafts.

## *Reflective practice for editing: The opposite of writing*

Now you have read this chapter, it's time to reflect on what you want to take forward and put into practice.

Reflect on the following questions:

- How does moving from the small details to the big picture make you feel? Does it help you see the forest for the trees (4.1), or does everything feel less coherent? What strategies can you put in place to return to coherence?
- How does being critical about your own writing make you feel? Do you feel empowered to identify gaps and inconsistencies and fix them? Or does it feel negative and critical of your writing ability? What strategies can you put in place to feel more competent at writing?
- How does thinking about your text from a reader's perspective make you feel? Do you feel excited about sharing your work with others, or does it feel like you are estranged or distanced from your own work? What strategies can you put in place to feel confident and generous?

You might use reflection tools like journaling, talking to a colleague, or mindfulness activities (discussed in Chapters 1–3 and Section 4.2).

# Polishing
## Making your thesis shine

Once you have the right sections and paragraphs, you can start working on whether you have the right sentences, the right words, the right formatting and punctuation. Getting down to the details a copy editor is responsible for requires laser-focus and attention to detail. It's also a chance to make your writing shine.

Copy editing or polishing makes your writing conform to the rules of dictionaries, grammars and style guides. Because there are so many rules, machine tools can be built to help with this stage of the writing process, including spell checkers, grammar checkers, computer translation and reference software. Some universities will allow you to hire an external copy editor for your PhD, because this does not contribute to your intellectual contribution, only to your presentation.

However, you can't fully outsource your copy editing to another person. The machine tools and copy editors can help flag where your work may be unclear or seems to be incorrect, but you are the expert on the extensive technical and unusual information in your PhD thesis. Errors can be added inadvertently, something that becomes more likely the more original or unusual your content is, especially with technical language, names or foreign language words. You will still need to read over the material with a critical eye and ensure it still accurately reflects your research and ideas.

Do not merge or reverse the editing and polishing stages. Restructuring or reordering your material may impact your topic sentences, word choice, tenses and referencing (especially in fields where the first citation is formatted differently). Be kind to yourself and your research deadlines by restructuring at the macro-level (whole of thesis or chapter) and the meso-level

DOI: 10.4324/9781003307945-7

133

(paragraphs and sections) first, and only then move on to the micro-level (sentences and words).

## 6.1 A mindfulness practice for polishing: Putting your copy editor hat on

Philosopher Edward de Bono suggests that you can put on different thinking caps to look at a problem from different angles: de Bono proposes one 'hat' that focuses on information and facts; another looks for positives; another looks for risks and problems; a different hat considers hunches and feelings; and yet another hat considers creativity and new possibilities. Thinking about anything using these different approaches in parallel can help us to make progress and solve complex challenges.

You will swap 'hats' often throughout your PhD. In the reading and thinking stage, your brain's task is to understand facts, ideas and data. In the planning stage, you need to be creative and optimistic about the work you will write in the future. In the writing stage, you need to be generating new words and explaining information for the first time. In the editing stage, you need to take a big-picture view and look for big conceptual problems.

The copy editor needs to focus solely on getting the text into its final, polished state. The research and analysis is already complete. The sections are all in the draft in the right order. All the data, ideas and information is correct. A copy editor does not have anything to say about the structure, scope or value of your work.

How might you get into this majorly different headspace? Here is an exercise you might try.

Put on your 'copy editor' hat (this might be a real hat or an imaginary one!)

Say:

- I am now a copy editor!
- I am rule-bound, conforming to the style guidelines in matters of formatting and presentation.
- Every section must have a beginning, middle and end.
- Every paragraph must have a topic sentence.
- Every sentence must make sense, following directly from the sentences before, and leading to the sentences coming after.

- Every word must be grammatically correct and correctly spelled. If the meaning is unclear, I will look it up in the dictionary.

This is not very creative work. It's about looking up details in dictionaries, grammars and style guides. It's about making sure that you lay out your captions in exactly the same way throughout the thesis. It's about replacing all those dashes and ellipses with academic punctuation, and removing all those notes to yourself.

This might be your favourite part of the process, because it's possible to get it right. It might be your least favourite part of the process, because you prefer the open-ended or creative parts of the work. Either way, it's helpful to put on the copy editor hat, and then remember to take it off when you need to move to the next stage of the process.

---

**Options**

You might find moving spaces helps you move headspaces. If that's the case, you may find Section 7.2 useful.

---

**Notes**

Edward de Bono. *Six Thinking Hats*. Penguin, 2008.

---

## 6.2 A physical wellbeing practice for polishing: Five ways to stretch

An important part of a polishing draft is making sure your work is consistent across the whole document, which can mean long days of sitting in front of a computer in a consistent position: upright on a chair, arms reaching forward to my keyboard, eyes on the screen, hips and knees and ankles at 90 degrees to each other. This is an ergonomic, sustainable position that I can keep up for significant time boxes.

However, there is no one ideal posture that you should take and maintain for the full working day. A lot of posture advice is so focused on where your knees are that it isn't clear that you should only be in that position for a short while. The mandated university ergonomics training I recently had to undertake suggests you should sit for 20 minutes, stand for eight and move for two minutes in each half hour. Therefore, the best posture is actually a series of different positions.

In other parts of the writing cycle, I recommend moving to work in different spaces, but for the polishing stage, I find it's more helpful to incorporate regular stretches and then get back to my computer. I like stretches that make my limbs move in the opposite way to their typical desk position.

A good stretch should feel good. If you start wincing or holding your breath, it's a sign to back off. Try to unclench your jaw and breathe slowly through your nose, to expand the release and calm. If any of these poses isn't great for you—any other stretch you enjoy will be just as good, or check out the 'Options' section for adjustments.

**Side bends:** When you work at a desk, you typically don't do much movement side to side. Sitting in your computer chair, you can stretch your arms out wide. Turn your head and look at your right hand, and then pull your right hand up to the ceiling as you pull your left hand down towards the floor. Move your whole head and torso to tip one way. Then turn your head to gaze at your left hand, and sweep that up high, reversing the movement.

Repeat these as many times as you like to move your arms, shoulders, back, neck and eyes.

**Back twists (standing thoracic rotations):** Facing forward to a computer means you aren't doing a lot of rotations, so add in some twist stretches. Stand up, spread your arms out wide and look towards your right hand. Pull your right arm back, following it with your gaze, letting your left arm rotate forward. Swing your eyes to your left hand and pull it back behind you, letting the other hand pivot forward.

Repeat these as many times as you like to move your arms, shoulders, back, neck and eyes in another direction.

**Arm stretch backs (standing biceps stretch):** If you are reaching forward to your keyboard or paper draft, you can reverse your position by reaching backwards. Stand up and interlace your fingers behind your back. Keep your hands near the base of your spine, and push out to get your arms as long and straight as possible. Move your head in any way that feels good for you and see if that gives you a good feeling along your neck and shoulders.

This might stretch your chest and the front of your shoulders as well as your wrists.

**Wide-legged squat (*Mālāsana*, Garland pose):** I tend to sit with my legs crossed or parallel on a chair. This posture makes them move in the opposite direction. Stand with your legs wide apart, and slowly squat down as low as you can go. Squats move your ankles, calves and hips.

**Lying-forward back bends (*Bhujaṅgāsana*, Cobra pose):** Lie on your front on the floor, and then push yourself up by your arms until you come into a gentle back bend to reverse the desk position of your ankles, hips, back, shoulders and neck.

These stretches don't stop me from feeling tired at the end of the day, but they help me feel less pain and stiffness. Finishing a thesis is a slog, mentally and physically. Anything you can do to lighten the load is a massive help!

---

### Options

Obtain advice from your health professional before starting any exercise program and, as always, go gently.

Hold each stretch for as long as feels good to you. A good start is to try moving around in the stretch for between about 20 seconds and a few minutes. Any version of these stretches will be great. I've included the specific names if you want to find a picture or video online too.

You can do the standing stretches on a stool or the floor if that is more comfortable. Make the squat a bit easier by giving yourself a bolster or block to sit on, or a wall against your back.

Dial up Cobra pose by pushing up strongly through your arms, lifting your hipbones and knees off the ground, and coming into Upward Facing Dog (*Ūrdhva Mukha Śvānāsana*).

The more intense poses I use a lot are any kind of inversion (going upside down) and Saddle pose (*Supta Vīrāsana*, Reclining Hero pose). These may already be in your practice. Alternatively, Dianne Bondy provides accessible shoulder stand and bow variations you could explore (2019, pp. 172–173 and p. 211).

**Notes**

Dianne Bondy, *Yoga for Everyone: 50 Poses for Every Type of Body*. Dorling Kindersley, 2019.

A first version of this section was written for *Research Degree Insiders*: https://researchinsiders.blog/2020/12/23/the-5-stretches-that-kept-me-going-during-my-recent-final-book-edit/ and https://researchinsiders.blog/2022/07/28/whats-the-best-writing-posture/

## 6.3 How to polish: Different strategies

No part of the writing process is as well-documented as the polishing process. Because it is rule-bound, there are extensive rule books. Academic language, and the English language, also have rules and norms that can be described. You will have learned about spelling, grammar, punctuation and so on from the moment you learned to start reading and writing in English, so you will probably already have a range of techniques that you have been building up through your study and professional life.

In her survey of style guides, Helen Sword (2012) found that there was 'virtually unanimous' agreement in terms of:

- 'clarity, coherence, concision'
- 'short or mixed-length sentences'
- 'plain English'
- 'precision'
- 'active verbs'
- 'telling a story'.

(pp. 26–27)

So feel free to take the advice of any writing guide that you already enjoy on those points, whether the guide was originally aimed at school kids, business people, creative writers, or researchers.

However, the style guides do contain differences in terms of personal pronouns, voice, tone, and creativity, as well as specifics on how to format a reference or lay out your manuscript (see Section 6.3.3).

The polishing strategies in this book are focused on getting under the rules to understand the deep processes and structures of academic writing to help you polish with confidence and grace.

---

### Notes

Helen Sword, *Stylish Academic Writing*. Harvard University Press, 2012.

---

### Next Steps

For more practical and detailed advice on writing well in the polishing stage, see the advice on style guides in Section 6.3.2, or *How to Fix your Academic Writing Trouble, Your PhD Survival Guide* (particularly Chapter 10), and *Level Up Your Essays* (Chapters 6 and 7).

---

#### 6.3.1 Defamiliarizing techniques so you can see your work again

The first task in polishing your work is to read over every single word. After working through the outline, sections, paragraphs and chapters in the editing stage, you need to get right down into the tiny details in the polishing stage. Many people find that just reading over things one more time stops working after a while. Your eyes are too tired, and too familiar with the work, to catch big or small errors anymore. You have already planned, written and edited this draft, and on the screen, we tend to skim over text we are already very familiar with.

So the trick is to defamiliarize the text enough to be able to read the draft, and slow down enough to see all the details. Here are some options for getting to that place.

There is nothing quite like time to help you forget what you wrote, so you can read it as if for the first time. A critical distance break is helpful here (see Section 4.3.1). The bigger the project, and the longer you have been working on it, though, the longer the critical distance break needs to be. You probably don't have three months to get away from your thesis, so you can combine breaks with other defamiliarization techniques.

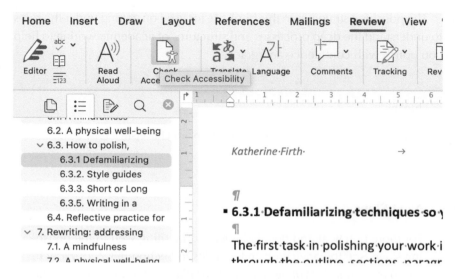

*Figure 6.1* Screenshot of MS Word 'Review' pane with the 'Read Aloud' button

A good way to see your writing anew is to change the way the writing looks. You can print out the draft or change the font, for example. These are very simple tricks, but they are extraordinarily effective.

One of the best ways to 'see' your words and sentences anew is to 'hear' them. Use text-to-voice or 'Read Aloud' tools to hear your draft. The pace of reading text aloud means you have to slow right down. It's impossible to skim or skip forward. Reading words aloud means you will catch missing words, repeated small words and wrong words. You will also catch missing commas and full stops, and sentences that are so long they don't make sense anymore.

Most people are more fluent at speaking and listening than they are at reading and writing, so you will find listening aloud helps polish your draft, whether English is a second language for you, or if you are a native English speaker who works out if the grammar is correct by whether it 'sounds right'.

You can achieve the same outcomes by reading your draft aloud, but it can become a strain for your eyes and voice. Computers don't get tired. You can give your tired eyes a break and use your ears instead. What's more, you don't have to sit at a desk while you listen to your draft. While listening to the computer say every word in your massive draft, you could be walking around the room, or lying on the floor doing your stretches. The computer can be interrupted to edit sentences, and then it's ready to start back up.

Defamiliarization also helps you combat boredom. We've been on this writing cycle for a long time, and this content is old information to you. Researchers search out new knowledge, so rehashing old knowledge isn't quite so much fun. But the polishing stage makes such a difference to the reader, so defamiliarization helps us have more energy and bandwidth to be generous to our future audience.

---

### Notes

Rakefet Ackerman and Murray Goldsmith, 'Metacognitive Regulation of Text Learning: On Screen Versus on Paper', *Journal of Experimental Psychology: Applied*, 17:1, 18–32. 2011.

Maura Pilotti, Martin Chodorow and Kendell C Thornton, 'Error Detection in Text: Do Feedback and Familiarity Help?', *The Journal of General Psychology*, 131:3, 242–267. 2004.

Paul T Rankin, 'The Importance of Listening Ability', *The English Journal*, 17:8, 623–630. 1928.

A first version of this section was written for *Research Degree Insiders*:

https://researchinsiders.blog/2020/02/27/three-secrets-in-msword-that-will-supercharge-your-productivity/

---

### Next Steps

There are lots of different options for voices, with different genders and regional accents. Select a voice that sounds friendly or is easy to listen to for you.

Defamiliarization is a way of putting on a different kind of 'thinking hat' (see Section 6.1), and of putting yourself more in the mindset of your reader (see Section 5.1).

Use stretches and other movements to keep you feeling well as you improve your writing (see Section 6.2).

---

#### 6.3.2 Style guides

There are so many books that give advice on how to write well (I personally have co-authored three others before this one!), but the most important book is your discipline's style guide. Obviously you will use a style guide to format your references, but they are useful for far more. Many people have never thought much about their style guide or used it for more than checking how to format a reference. But style guides reflect and create academic communities, so a deeper exploration of what a style guide is might help you as you develop your academic identity.

Style guides are often named after a university press (like Chicago), or a scholarly society (like APA [American Psychological Association] or MLA [Modern Languages Association]). Sometimes, there are regional differences: you are more likely to use MLA in the United States, but MHRA (Modern Humanities Research Association) in the United Kingdom. The North American guides tend to be much bigger books and more frequently updated: the *MLA Style Manual* (2021) is in its ninth edition in 37 years and has 400 pages, whereas the *MHRA Style Guide* (2013) is currently only in its third edition in 51 years and has just 120 pages.

Some styles have confusing names, for example 'Vancouver' style is based on *Citing Medicine* (2nd edition, 2015) from the National Library of Medicine in the United States, it refers to a numerical citation style used in medical research. Although the *Publication Manual of the American Psychological Association* (APA, 7th edition, 428 pages, 2020) might sound like a regional style used mostly in psychology, it is in fact the most common global style used across the sciences, as well as psychology and sociology research. 'Harvard' style does not refer to a specific style guide, but rather to a generic author-date referencing style (Chernin 1988). Oxford University Press uses a style guide called *New Hart's Rules*. Some style guides have a workbook or student textbook version, the most famous being *Turabian*, after Kate Turabian's *A Manual for Writers of Research Papers, Theses, and Dissertations* (7th edition, 2007, 470 pages). This is a student-friendly and much shorter version of the full *Chicago Manual of Style* (17th edition, 2018, 1146 pages).

Style guides are useful for the thousands of detailed questions that you need to have answers for in writing your PhD thesis: do I use single or double quote marks; when do I use a numeral (1) and when do I use a word (one); how do I number and format my subheadings; where do the captions for figures go? You do not have to make these decisions on your own, you just look them up in your style guide and save your decision-making powers for the many choices that have research impacts. If you have used the style guide, your supervisor and peer reviewers will also make far fewer corrections on your manuscript.

But wider questions of 'is this writing academic?' or 'am I allowed to write in this way?' might also be resolved by exploring your style guide. As the many pages and the frequent editions demonstrate, style guides cover way more than just referencing, and they are keeping up with advances in technology and society. In her book, *Stylish Academic Writing*, Helen Sword surveyed 100 articles in each of 10 disciplines, and a further 100 writing guides. She notes that science style guides often recommend the use of 'I' or 'we', especially for clarity or to show when a decision has been made. The *APA Publication Manual* has recommended using personal pronouns since 1974, she notes, and major science guides like the *ACS Style Guide*, the *AMA Manual* and the *CSE Manual* agree (p. 39). So if you have been told that personal pronouns 'aren't academic' or 'aren't used in science' or 'aren't objective', you can look up your style guide and find out if that's true.

Each university, journal and publisher will have further instructions on style, possibly called 'guidelines', 'author guides', 'information for authors' 'schedule for presentation' or 'formatting guide'. These will have details about practical questions like what to put in the title, how long to make the abstract, and what software to use to submit your work. The author instructions take precedence over the style guide if they come into conflict at any point. These instructions on style tend to get updated more frequently than the big style guides, so they can often have the answer to contemporary writing questions. For example, in *How to Fix your Academic Writing Trouble*, we used the gender-neutral singular 'they', both because we wanted to be inclusive, and because it was recommended by our publisher's guidelines (2018, p. 113).

The advice in the publisher's style guide can go well beyond details, and encompass big questions about audience, purpose and what is valued in 'good' writing. For example, *Nature*, one of the most competitive academic journals, has its own 'Formatting Guide', which goes well beyond how to format your paper. The guide also includes an extensive section on 'Readability':

> Contributions should therefore be written clearly and simply so that they are accessible to readers in other disciplines and to readers for whom English is not their first language. Thus, technical jargon should be avoided as far as possible and clearly explained where its use is unavoidable.

143

Your PhD thesis will typically be written primarily for a specialist audience of two or more expert examiners, demonstrating your understanding of the academic field in order to be approved to join that field as a peer. However, the 'style' of writing you need if you want to publish from your thesis in a high-impact journal might be quite different. Therefore, the place you will find out about what to change will be in the style guide.

Your style guide can support your writing in an unexpected number of ways. It can give you clarity about what to do to achieve academic style. It can resolve conflicts with supervisors and peer reviewers who might have outdated preferences. And in many cases, the style guides are interested in ethical, inclusive writing that does good in the world.

## Notes

*Publication Manual of the American Psychological Association: The Official Guide to APA Style*, 7th Edition. American Psychological Association, 2019.

*The Chicago Manual of Style*, 17th Edition. University of Chicago Press, 2017.

Eli Chernin, 'The "Harvard System": A Mystery Dispelled', *British Medical Journal*, 297:6655, 1062–1063. 1988.

'Formatting Guide', *Nature*. https://www.nature.com/nature/for-authors/formatting-guide

*MLA Handbook*, 9th Edition. The Modern Language Association of America, 2021.

Karen Patrias, *Citing Medicine: The NLM Style Guide for Authors, Editors, and Publishers*, edited by Daniel L Wendling (technical editor). Department of Health and Human Services, National Institutes of Health, US National Library of Medicine, 2007.

Helen Sword, *Stylish Academic Writing*. Harvard University Press, 2012.

Kate L Turabian, *A Manual for Writers of Research Papers, Theses, and Dissertations: Chicago Style for Students and Researchers*, 9th edition, revised by Wayne C Booth, Gregory G Colomb, Joseph M Williams, Joseph Bizup, William T FitzGerald, and the University of Chicago Press editorial staff. University of Chicago Press, 2018.

Anne Waddingham, *New Hart's Rules: The Oxford Style Guide*, 2nd Edition. Oxford University Press, 2014.

### 6.3.3 Short or long sentences?

I hear a lot of conflicting advice on how to write sentences, and I bet you do too. Should you write short sentences, because they are easier to read? Should you write longer sentences because they sound more academic? Should you write a careful mix of sentences, because that creates good flow? None of the usual advice is bad—you just need to develop good judgement about when to apply it.

The research is interesting on shorter sentences versus longer sentences. Students rated simpler writing as 'more intelligent' in a study by Oppenheimer in 2005, whereas a famous study by Armstrong in 1980 found that faculty and journal reviewers associated more prestige with writing that was more complex. So audience and purpose matters.

Shorter, simpler sentences are best, sometimes. Shorter, simpler sentences are easier and quicker to read. It's less likely that your reader will get confused or bored if your sentences are short and snappy. In a shorter, simpler sentence, it's less likely that you will need to navigate complex decisions about whether to use commas or semicolons. It's easy to make common mistakes in long sentences like changing tense halfway through, or not keeping all your verbs agreeing with the main noun.

Shorter sentences are best for action items, documentation or methods where people have to follow your instructions. A clear, direct sentence is likely to lead to a clear, direct action! Short, simple sentences are fantastic in emails, blogs and press releases, anything that people expect to skim-read in a hurry.

However, shorter sentences have limits. A straightforward sentence excludes the option to include extra information to give nuance to the main sentence. Short sentences can sound brusque, over-confident, or too general. Academic writing is often talking about information that is complex, indefinite or super-specific: in other words, it is not simple, short and straightforward. Simple, short, straightforward sentences might cut out much of the information that you need in order to be correct. Don't value brevity over accuracy, politeness, or formality.

Shorter sentences are less information-dense than longer sentences, so they may not work as well when you have a lot of information to convey but only a limited number of words. Every sentence needs a subject (a noun that the sentence is about), and a main verb (what the subject is doing), and you need to repeat this for every new sentence. A lot of short sentences therefore use up valuable words in abstracts and grant applications with very limited word counts.

Some people rewrite short, straightforward sentences to be longer and more flowery. If the sentence is just fine being short, leave it short. Don't use unnecessary 'filler' words just to bump up your word count, you need that space for important information elsewhere. However, dense sentences are more difficult to read, and your reader can get tired, so don't overuse them. Only use complex sentences where your ideas merit it. Your reader might feel resentful if they are forced to read lots of challenging sentences when your information isn't worth it.

So, longer, more complex sentences are best, sometimes. Longer sentences allow you to cram a lot of information into a small number of words. Long sentences are often needed when explaining complex theories, introducing uncertain or incomplete knowledge, or mobilizing criticism of important scholars or common knowledge. Longer sentences allow you to include more information and more context. You have room to add descriptions, more data, or a complementary point of view. For example, you might need to add 'hedging' or 'caution' phrases to avoid overstating certainty; include definitions or translations in the text; or supply more context, data or nuance to be more exact. Nuance, cautiousness, politeness and detail all require more words in the sentence. Inclusive language often requires more words, the capaciousness of our inclusion often demands more capacious sentences.

Many of the longest sentences I find in journal articles are very efficient with words. List sentences, for example, might be 50-plus words long, but allow the writer to cover a lot of ground with fewer words. Or a long sentence in a literature review might summarize a big argument, to show that the author is familiar with the ideas and contribution of a body of scholarship, without getting distracted from the main topic.

Other scholars often write in longer sentences. So you may want to write like them, to show you belong. If you are in a discipline where you regularly quote the work of other researchers, the quotes are likely to be long too.

And medium sentences are best, sometimes. A typical academic sentence is 25–35 words, and has a main clause and one to two extra clauses. If you go through a journal article, you'll notice that the majority of sentences look about the same. I counted sentences in a range of articles, and found they tended to range from 18–30 words.

A mix of sentence lengths is best, sometimes. Gary Provost gave the famous advice about varying your sentence length:

Write with a combination of short, medium, and long sentences. Create a sound that pleases the reader's ear. Don't just write words. Write music.

(1972/1985, 5.4)

Provost was discussing creative writing: 'This sentence has five words. Here are five more words. Five-word sentences are fine. But several together become monotonous' (5.4). In academic writing, we honestly don't care how long your sentences are, in terms of their longness, but we do care if they are the right length for the job. In academic writing, we put the function of your writing first. Academic writing can be dull, obscure or technical, because sometimes the information we are looking for is technical, and only interesting to a small group of fellow experts. That is a feature, not a bug!

So you need to be able to write short, medium and long sentences, but mostly you need to be able to write the right sentence for the information you want to convey. This produces sentences that are considerate of your reader and accurately reflect your research.

## Notes

J Scott Armstrong, 'Unintelligible Management Research and Academic Prestige', *Interfaces*, 10:2, 80–86. 1980.

DM Oppenheimer, 'Consequences of Erudite Vernacular Utilized Irrespective of Necessity: Problems with Using Long Words Needlessly', *Applied Cognitive Psychology*, 20, 139–156. 2006.

Gary Provost, *100 Ways to Improve your Writing*. Penguin, 1972/1985.

A first version of this section was written for *Research Degree Insiders*: https://researchinsiders.blog/2021/07/22/shorter-sentences-longer-sentences/

## Next Steps

For basic information about writing sentences, see *How to Fix your Academic Writing Trouble*. Find out more about clear sentences on pp. 62–67; 'parataxis' and 'hypotaxis' (short disconnected and long highly-connected sentences) on pp. 97–99; filler words on pp. 101–104; and 'hedging' on pp. 119–122.

### 6.3.4 Writing in a second language

Students who don't speak English as their first language are often very worried about writing up their PhD thesis. And many supervisors are also worried about the writing of their English as a Second or Further Language PhD candidates. But in the literature, we contest the 'deficit' model (Smit 2012; Kahu and Nelson 2018). It is not true that if English isn't your first language, you must be less likely to succeed. You're actually doing great. In fact, international students pass at the same rate as local students and often complete more swiftly (Torka 2020). So the data says you will do absolutely fine. You can also benefit from these techniques if academic English is a new way of writing for you.

The most important point is to stop worrying. When we read your work, it's generally really good. To get into a PhD program in an English-speaking country, you have to have demonstrated you already have a really high level of English. We set this hurdle, because we believe it is the level you need to succeed in your degree. You've proven you meet the criteria, so you meet the criteria. No one is writing perfect academic texts—we're all compromising and doing our best and struggling and being just good enough a lot of the time. You aren't held to a higher standard because English isn't your first language!

Supervisors who don't have expertise in developing writers often default to commenting on things they know how to fix, and blaming the language barrier, plus correcting grammar and spelling is easy. Helping people with structure, developing new concepts, or understanding theory, are hard. Yet unclear, error-prone or bad writing is frequently due to a lack of structure, or a sign that you still don't understand the concepts and data yet. The problem is often not one of fluency, but of research progress. This is why early years writing is often very weak, because the project still needs another three years of work to be properly developed.

Writing a PhD is hard. You need to learn a mass of high-level, complex writing skills. Your native English-speaking peers also have to learn these new skills—and they will be finding it hard too. You might not be using language correctly, or not understand a term fully, because you are still coming to understand the complex ideas that a word or term stands for. The problem isn't that you don't have good enough English for 'actor network theory', 'relativity' or 'translocalism', but rather that these terms represent contested, unclear, difficult or developing fields of knowledge.

All in all, if you are finding it hard to write a PhD in English, you are doing it right—you are learning, engaging with issues, and developing new skills to be able to write a book-length, original, scholarly work!

That doesn't mean there aren't some strategies that are particularly helpful to ESL PhD candidates. I'll share five techniques that candidates tell me are useful to them:

1. What are your most common errors? Typically, much of the trouble is caused by a few small errors that happen frequently. Common examples are subject-verb agreements or using 'the'. The issue with your writing probably isn't 'everything', it is likely to be the same small things over and over again.
   - Make a list of the things.
   - Look up how to do the things correctly online or in a textbook.
   - Do a read-through just for that error. This will involve going over your writing more than once, but each read-through will be fast.
   - As you practise getting it right, you will build good habits so you will slowly write less error-prone text.

2. Improve your academic English in ten minutes a week. Spend ten minutes every week reading a well-written book, article or thesis in your discipline for style, vocabulary and structure rather than content or ideas.
   - How do they introduce their argument? What words do they use to signpost or make judgements? Are their sentences long or short? How do they show when they disagree? What goes in the introduction?
   - Build up an idea of what is normal. You are expected to write using the same words and forms, so borrow their vocabulary and phrases.

3. Practise writing regularly. If your PhD doesn't give a lot of writing opportunities before your third year, find other ways to keep up your writing skills.
   - Keep a reflective journal as you research or find a pen pal in your field at a conference and write to them each week.
   - Join the editorial board of an academic journal, write for your student newspaper.
   - Keep writing, otherwise, you may notice your skills go backwards.

4. Write your drafts mostly in English, but if you get stuck on a word, put it down in your first language. If you've ever listened to bilingual people talk, you'll hear them do this in conversation all the time.
   - Students report that writing in their first language and translating it into English ended up being much more work.
   - Instead, write in a polyglot style for your first draft, you can go through and translate all the individual words later.
   - Don't spend too long looking for the best word. A clear, simple word is good. A close-enough word is a good enough start. As you develop as a writer, or use feedback from your supervisor, you can make other word choices later if you need to.
5. And finally, long sentences, fancy words and jargon don't make you 'sound academic'. If scholars use those techniques, we are using them because they help us explain our thinking better.
   - You will 'sound academic' when you describe academic thoughts: a strong argument, critical analysis, deep insight, expert judgment.

In conclusion, people writing their thesis in a second language should feel confident they can and will succeed.

## Notes

We have better data about fee types than about language background, so the data can be messy.

Ella R Kahu and Karen Nelson, 'Student Engagement in the Educational Interface: Understanding the Mechanisms of Student Success', *Higher Education Research & Development*, 37:1, 58–71. 2018.

Renee Smit, 'Towards a Clearer Understanding of Student Disadvantage in Higher Education: Problematising Deficit Thinking', *Higher Education Research & Development*, 31:3, 369–380. 2012.

Marc Torka, 'Change and Continuity in Australian Doctoral Education: PhD Completion Rates and Times (2005–2018)', *The Australian Universities' Review*, 62:2, 69–82. 2020.

Swales and Feak have good vocabulary and phrase examples in *Academic Writing for Graduate Students* (1994/2012).

A first version of this section was written for *Research Degree Insiders* and published as 'Writing a PhD in Your Second Language: Seven Reasons You're Doing Great and Five Ways to do Even Better' on the *LSE Impact Blog*, 2017:

https://blogs.lse.ac.uk/impactofsocialsciences/2017/12/21/writing-a-phd-in-your-second-language-seven-reasons-youre-doing-great-and-five-ways-to-do-even-better/

## Reflective practice for polishing: Soothing or gritty?

Now you have read this chapter, it's time to reflect on what you want to take forward and put into practice.

When you are making a piece of wood smooth, you use a rough surface like sandpaper to gradually remove any unwanted rough edges. The same concept applies to polishing your thesis.

Reflect on the following questions:

1. Creating something smooth, with regular gentle movements, can feel soothing. Does polishing your writing feel soothing to you?
2. For other people, the roughness of the sandpaper, the grating sound it makes, and getting covered in sawdust feels irritating and gritty. Does polishing your writing make you feel irritated?
3. This stage also encourages you to pay close attention to uneven details and small flaws. Does this attention to the detail of what needs to be smoothed away feel soothing or gritty to you?
4. If you answered 'gritty' to the preceding questions, what is your strategy for self-care after you have finished this irritating task? (Look back at what you said in the reflection for Chapter 4, it might give you some ideas, or you might want to add some extra steps into your closing ritual for these situations!)

You might use reflection tools like journaling, talking to a colleague, or mindfulness activities (discussed in Chapters 1–3 and Section 4.2).

# Rewriting

## 7 Addressing feedback from yourself and others

No project as long and complex as a PhD will be written with just one draft. You will go over each chapter multiple times, as will your supervisor. You will get feedback from reviewers, committees and conferences, and each time you will need to revise your work. Even after submission, your thesis will often need revisions, and then will require even more rewriting to get it ready to be published.

The revisions might send you back to any previous stage of the writing cycle. You may need to do more research and analysis, or more reading. You may have to write more sections. You may need to make small or large structural edits. You may need to ensure all the sections are in the same font. This moment of needing to begin the cycle again can be challenging for writers, and it is at this moment some choose to abandon the writing project altogether. It is a big shift from other forms of writing such as coursework assessment, where you rarely rewrite, or professional writing, where rewriting tends to be more collegial.

You must expect to rewrite, and so it helps if you can learn to value it, and not feel like that means there is anything wrong with your writing. This chapter gives strategies to thrive in this crucial part of a sustainable writer's life.

Experienced academic writers know that fewer drafts don't make for better writing. These days, I expect to go through the full writing cycle at least twice before handing a manuscript to a beta reader, again before it goes out to reviewers and again after comments from my editor. I will review it again after the copy editor has worked on it, and then after the layout team has done the formatting. And this is assuming it's a straightforward project! I'll do more drafts if it's co-authored, or we get a 'revise and resubmit' from the peer reviewers, or if the material is complicated or sensitive. As an emerging

DOI: 10.4324/9781003307945-8

academic writer, you are likely to need a few extra times around the cycle as you find your voice, define your scope and work out how to be a researcher. But you will always need to face the rewriting, no matter how experienced you get.

## 7.1 A mindfulness practice for rewriting: A gratitude practice for your writing

You will need to write an Acknowledgements section in your thesis, and you can have fun working out who you will thank and how you'll include acknowledgements in your thesis. But you might also want to make a less formal, less constrained, more honest version.

Here, for example, is my gratitude list. It includes some things that have been published in Acknowledgement sections and quite a few that haven't.

These are things I'm grateful for, now and as a PhD student.

I am grateful for:

- A supervisor who got what I was trying to say, and gave me tools to say it more clearly.
- Co-authors who get what I'm trying to say, and give me space to work out how to say it well.
- Editors who get what I'm trying to say, and fix my work so it actually says it.
- Peer reviewers who don't get what I'm trying to say, and give me feedback so I know what's not communicating.
- Students who tell me that what I say changes their lives.
- Computers who take the work of spellchecking, footnoting, sharing and saving my work, and make it instant and invisible.
- Computer catalogues, which are so much better than the old paper catalogues for 99% of searches. I love you all, but maybe WorldCat the most.
- Librarians who put relevant books together on shelves, so when I go to pick up one book for my research, I find another dozen nearby.
- Archivists who spent months digitizing material, so when I need it, it's there in seconds.
- Wikipedia editors who summarize a topic and point me to the most relevant information.
- Colleagues who are delighted to grab a coffee or find time for a chat.

- Scholarships, prizes and grants that offered me the chance to study, travel, buy books and just live.
- Other scholars with generous footnotes that explain a new field to me, and publishers who make space for generous footnotes.
- Shut Up and Write buddies over the years who helped me get some writing done when the writing was hard to get to.
- The members of my reading groups who keep me up to date in the field.
- My beautiful walnut desk, and the view of leaves and sky outside my study window.
- The non-human writing companions (particularly the black cats) who have only interrupted my work in ways that provoked creativity.
- Coffee and herbal tea and nice water, which help me get into the writing zone.
- Heating and cooling and windows that open so I write in comfort more often.
- The people who write and perform and record the amazing music that gets me in a writing mood every time.
- Everyone who ever posted a video explainer about how to move and stretch after I've spent too many hours at my desk.
- The people who buy, read or review my books and blog, who inspire me to keep going.
- Students who ask searching questions, admit their writing challenges, and come up with innovative solutions, who make me a better teacher.

I am grateful for so many other things, but this is a first list. It was so much fun writing this list! You should have a go yourself, because every researcher deserves to have fun.

A gratitude list doesn't mean you don't have aspects of the research degree that are difficult or horrible. But human brains are better at noticing problems because it helps us solve them, and the problems around us are obvious (Rozin and Royzman 2001). A gratitude list just helps you make the good stuff equally obvious.

To be clear, I have also sat down to write a gratitude list in the past and found it consisted of something like 'I have a job, for now' and 'I work with some great people, who are leaving soon'. That has led to me realizing I needed to radically change my life. That is also a useful exercise.

A PhD is a wonderful opportunity to be granted the space and permission to take a few years to learn, think and focus on an area you are deeply interested in. Research degrees are often personalized, exploratory and financially supported. You get a supervisor just for your project! You get to answer questions you are seriously curious about! Maybe you got a scholarship! Wow!

I hope your research gratitude list is full and overflowing. And if it's not, maybe it's time to see what you can do to make things better and more joyful.

---

**Notes**

Paul Rozin and Edward B Royzman, 'Negativity Bias, Negativity Dominance, and Contagion', *Personality and Social Psychology Review*, 5:4, 296–320. 2001.

---

## 7.2 A physical wellbeing practice for rewriting: Don't keep sitting in the same old chair

By the time you have got to the rewriting stage, you have been working on this draft for a long time. If you have a desk where you typically work, then your body and brain will have a well-established habit of associating your draft with that furniture (Clear, 2018). You'll have not only physical habits, but also habits of mind and habits of writing. It's going to be at least the sixth time you have gone over this content by now, since you have already thought about it, planned it, written it, edited it and polished it. It should all be feeling very familiar, maybe even a bit boring.

Rewriting requires a significant shake-up of those habits. If something was obvious or easy or unavoidable, then it would already be in the draft. You need to rewrite to add or address things that were missing or didn't work the first time around. So it's time to shake things up.

One useful way to get into another headspace is to change your physical space. Go to a different café. Take your writing from the desk to the sofa. Work in the library. Sit outside under a tree. Try working standing up, or lying on the floor.

Personally, I like to research, think and plan in a library. My favourite is the big dome in the State Library of Victoria, with embossed-leather desks on long carrels radiating out like spokes around the reading room. I like to type the first draft at my home desk. I like to edit on paper, with a pencil, often at the dining room table or on the sofa. I rewrite with my papers and laptop spread out across the big spare-room bed, with lots of pillows and cushions to make it soft and comfortable.

Some people like to book themselves in for a writing retreat at this stage, either alone in a hotel room or at an organized group event. You might switch from typing to voice-to-text here, or vice versa. You might change location every couple of hours to keep yourself motivated and moving.

Be as extreme or extravagant as you would like. You have already experimented with multiple different writing strategies through this book, so you know what can work for you. Use that knowledge or try out something new that you've always wanted to do.

---

**Options**

Section 3.2 gives you lots of options for places where you could work.

If you can only work in one chair for health reasons, think about changing something up about the chair you are working in, like a different cushion, or move the chair to another part of the house.

---

**Notes**

James Clear, *Atomic Habits: An Easy & Proven Way to Build Good Habits & Break Bad Ones.* Penguin, 2018. See Chapter 6.

---

## 7.3 How to rewrite: Different strategies

Rewriting will draw on all the different kinds of strategies you have already used in this book. You might need to go back to the literature or the data, and rethink. You might need to write new text. You might need to take some time away from the draft to get critical distance and perspective. You might need to restructure sections. You might have to dive into the details and sort out copy edits.

It might be that a strategy I recommended earlier in the book wasn't what you needed then, but it might come into its own now that you need to go back and try again.

You might also have to rethink how to track your progress. Rewriting can massively improve the quality of your writing but end up not looking much different in terms of how many words are in your draft, or what sections are complete. Think of a way to count the quality of words, not just the number (see Sections 2.4.1 and 3.4).

This section therefore deals more specifically with the wellbeing challenges of rewriting. You have realized or been told that your writing isn't good enough yet, even though you have already done so much really wonderful and hard work on it. That's tough and tiring, but it's also a sign you have made progress and are making progress. Keep up the good work!

### 7.3.1 Understanding feedback

Feedback is complex and multifactorial. It can identify problems with your ideas, analysis, reading, scope, writing or structure. So it can be hard for you or your reader to identify what is the cause and what is the symptom. Issues of grammar may be polishing errors, or foundational comprehension errors. Issues of structure might reflect incomplete editing, or the lack of an argument. Feedback also includes corrections where you made a mistake, suggestions, and the identification of problems that the reader has no idea how you might solve. Feedback is presented all at once, so your job is to be critical in your response to feedback.

As an emerging researcher-writer, your early months are often full of instructive feedback about where you could improve your drafts: maybe clarity, conciseness, tone, grammar or structure. You dutifully take note of the comments, and work to improve. But as you develop as a writer, you will need to learn to distinguish between the different kinds of 'corrections'. For example, some corrections should just go into your chapter verbatim, when what you have written is wrong and the comment is right. In this case, you should just retype what the supervisor has written. This is the most straightforward kind.

Sometimes, the corrections are actually only suggestions. Perhaps your supervisor comments that you would improve the structure of the chapter by swapping two sections, but when you sit down and try to do it, it makes things worse. Then you should obviously decide not to implement the changes, but instead make a note of why you decided against it. Sometimes, the corrections are more about identifying an issue. When the comments are strongly disagreeing with something that you haven't actually claimed, for example, rather than worry about the fact that the comments aren't fair, notice that you weren't sufficiently clear and obvious. Go back and explain it better so the next reader won't make the same mistake.

Supervisors are often very busy, and trying to fit in large chunks of difficult reading on top of their day job may mean that their comments are quick, semi-legible, and reactive. Often, the feedback is less of a book review, and more just annotations and reactions. A lot of feedback annotations are just notes to self about what worked or didn't, or in response to a quick proof-read. It's much easier to copy edit than it is to give deep structural formative feedback. It's also much easier to only comment on what wasn't quite right.

Challenging feedback can cause anxiety, confusion and resentment. You might take the feedback personally or be looking for reassurance and not get it. Or you might have a very harsh view of your own writing, and the feedback only exacerbates it. If any of these negative feelings are occurring, it makes it hard to productively turn the comments into the necessary revisions and to write the next draft. So exploring your mindset around feedback can be productive and generative.

On a practical level, you can be proactive in seeking and framing feedback in ways that are helpful for you. Ask for specific kinds of feedback and match the kind of feedback to your supervisor's strength as an editor. For example, 'Can you give me high-level general feedback as to whether the research direction seems sensible?' or 'Can you please do a careful final read to check I haven't made any typos?' It is your supervisor's job to help you produce a text that external examiners will pass, and their feedback should be helping you to understand what is expected of submitted work. Ask specifically for advice on what you need to pass. Don't ask for generic advice about making your writing 'better', try to find out *explicitly* what you need to pass your thesis.

You can respond to feedback with further questions and comments. Follow up with specific questions about the feedback when you meet your supervisor afterwards. For example, 'I notice there are a lot of corrections here about spelling and punctuation, would you prefer to get drafts only when they are highly polished?' You can also respond to feedback by demonstrating that you understand their point, but you disagree and can explain why. You can use second opinions, style guides, or evidence that you tried it and it didn't work. You should always offer an alternative solution, though.

Your supervisor is not the only person who can give you feedback. Get a writing buddy, mentor, coach, academic skills advisor, copy editor, and/or other experts to read your work at different stages. Each reader will provide a different kind of feedback, which will help you to see how different readers experience your writing.

Save yourself the obvious annoyances. Include the page numbers. Use spell check. Avoid that thing that you know annoys your supervisor. If your draft is at a very early, rough stage, perhaps submit just the introduction, or a report of the work you have done.

Trust the positive feedback. It's important not to skip over the praise. If your supervisor wrote, 'This all looks on track' or 'Good work' or gave you some ticks, then you are doing great. Many candidates worry when they don't get a lot of feedback on their drafts. In my experience, supervisors trust good candidates to get on with it. If your supervisor is happy with your work, you are probably doing fine. Ask around to the other candidates working with your supervisor. If some people are getting lots of very detailed feedback and rigorous rewrites, and you are getting 'this is great, keep it up', then you are likely doing really well. Your supervisor knows that you are successfully transitioning to becoming an independent scholar.

More importantly, though, positive feedback often identifies where you should learn from yourself. I now try to frame my positive feedback to students as 'this is great, do more of it'. While it's important to write in a way that avoids mistakes, it's probably more important to write in a way that portrays your ideas as convincing, exciting, or original.

Learning what readers enjoy and appreciate is essential to writing success. A computer can tell you if you have spelled a word wrong, but only another human can tell you that you have made their day or changed their mind with your writing. So when you do get praise, cherish it, but also learn from it. Write out specific comments about what you do well. Identify common words or themes. Maybe your academic writing is careful, comprehensive, elegant, or insightful at its best. Note it down and start to do more of it.

Hopefully this will help you next time you get feedback from your supervisor, to help make your writing better, and help you progress towards getting that thesis-thing done! This understanding of feedback, and the requirement for critical, creative and positive approaches to the comments you might get on your writing, will help power your rewriting.

**Notes**

A first version of this section was written for *Research Degree Insiders*: https://researchinsiders.blog/2021/03/18/is-the-thing-you-need-to-learn-from-feedback-how-to-accept-praise/ and https://researchinsiders.blog/2015/09/13/what-your-supervisor-means/

**Next Steps**

There's a lot more to feedback than this little section can address. Inger, Shaun and I wrote an entire book, *How to Fix Your Academic Writing Trouble*, all about understanding the feedback supervisors typically give, explaining what they really mean and how to put it into practice.

### 7.3.2 Dealing with failures

A PhD involves a lot of 'failures'. If none of your experiments fail, your supervisor never gives constructive criticism, and all your articles are published immediately without changes, then I'd worry that your project wasn't really a PhD! If you are working on complex, cutting-edge scholarship, with a supportive and engaged supervisor, and publishing in quality peer-reviewed journals, then you will definitely experience times when things don't work, and you need to build that into your timelines and get used to it, because that's supposed to be part of the process. It's normal to have articles rejected, even more than once. It's normal not to always get your proposal to that international conference accepted. It's normal to have to apply for lots of jobs before you get hired.

It's part of the experimental method of creating new knowledge that you might not find what you were expecting. As we push the boundaries of what is known, our methods, conceptual frameworks, language or models might stop working. As we try things out, explore, and problem-solve, we are likely to have times when we don't have answers yet. And when we work with people, systems, diseases or animals, it's likely that they will surprise us with unexpected results that challenge our established ways of understanding them. That's what research should be, that's how you make an original contribution to knowledge.

Some situations might look like 'failures', but actually be the right decision for you. If you quit your PhD for a good reason, take a leave of absence or go part-time, that might be due to a career or life success. Or perhaps you are prioritizing your physical or mental health or community for a time.

But there are also life-altering failures. A rejection of a publication, or even a significant delay, might mean you miss out on being shortlisted for a role. You might not get funding that enables you to continue your research—in fact, the stats suggest it's highly likely you won't get a major research grant. You might not get an academic job—in fact, the stats suggest that it's likely that you won't get an ongoing academic job, even if you do publish and get grants and take those postdoc positions. Rewriting is often when people recognize the gap between the writing work that still needs to happen and the likely benefits for your life and career.

These failures may be systemic and not at all your fault. I graduated with my PhD in the middle of the Global Financial Crisis. Everything got cancelled, and the job market cratered. I pivoted to academic skills, and as a humanities scholar, I was able to continue to research as long as I had a library card. Slowly I built my own research and writing community, and have a parallel 'alt-ac' career. My peers took a range of equally messy paths to try to stay in research. The more precarious your current position, the more a failure is going to impact your ability to keep going. Not everyone can afford to work part-time, or move around the world for short-term contracts, or have extended periods between contracts. Not every discipline allows you to find a way to do the work anyway.

Such failures, though, are not the end of the story. PhD candidates are resilient, persistent, creative, practical and great problem-solvers. Use your data collection and analysis skills to get a realistic idea about grants, jobs, salaries and options for you ahead of time. Resilience needs a buffer, so use your candidature time to build in extra capacity. Use your networking and communication skills to explore how you can build communities that will support and enable your ongoing writing. Use your creativity, curiosity and bravery to explore what other options there are beyond the university. Even academic-career-ending failures are not the end of your career.

The stats also tell us that two years out from your PhD, you have probably found something that is meaningful, challenging and exciting. You are using your skills and being recognized for it at work. Maybe you are working in a field closely related to your PhD, maybe you are using your transferable skills, or maybe you have started on another adventure to learn new skills or build new projects or explore new ideas.

Whatever you are doing, failing doesn't make you a failure. The wellbeing strategies you have put in place for when the writing is going well are even more important when things go wrong.

---

### Notes

The stats: QILT (Quality Indicators for Learning and Teaching): Graduate Outcomes Survey - *Longitudinal* (GOS-L) 2022 https://www.qilt.edu.au/surveys/graduate-outcomes-survey---longitudinal-(gos-l) (data for Australia)

Peta Freestone wrote about potentially quitting her PhD in *Your PhD Survival Guide*, Chapter 13.

A first version of this section was written for *Times Higher Education*: 'Thinking about quitting your PhD? Maybe that's the right decision' *Times Higher Education* 2022 https://www.timeshighereducation.com/campus/thinking-about-quitting-your-phd-maybe-thats-right-decision

---

### Next Steps

Deploying a growth mindset (see Section 1.3.3) *could help you explore which failures are chances to learn or develop.*

---

### 7.3.3 Dealing with perfectionism

Right now, perfectionism might be a huge challenge for you. Perhaps it won't let you finish anything. It prevents you from starting anything. You can't tell the difference between 'slightly imperfect' and 'absolutely shitty': leading you either to beat yourself up over tiny flaws in your excellent writing; or to hand in really early and unfinished writing to your supervisor, who then hands it back with lots of criticism.

Perfectionism means you won't listen when your supervisor says, 'This is great work, and you write really well'. You won't listen when they say, 'You're on track', or 'This should be in an article.' It means you stayed up all night going over what they meant when they said, 'your sentences are too long', or 'I think you need to add a few more references here'. Maybe you are trapped in the perfect sentence vortex of doom.

But there is a way out. And smart, self-motivated people with high standards, like PhD students, are the best people to take advantage of it.

Many people kind of accept that perfectionism is a flaw, but in an 'actually, this is a strength' way, so you're not going to change, really, because you secretly think that perfectionism helps you to do better. Some part of your hindbrain, and possibly large sections of your prefrontal cortex, truly believes that perfectionism is what has enabled you to reach the intellectual, professional and personal heights that you have.

But perfectionism is standing between you and success. Perfectionism isn't the same as 'having high standards', or 'caring about doing a good job', or 'getting the work done', or even 'being excellent'. It's a sickness, and it ruins academic careers.

I gave up on being perfect a while ago. Being perfect meant 99.9% was never good enough and always aiming for 150% was exhausting. I always (always!) tried to get things in early, under budget and exceeding targets, while being a charming, cheerful, team-playing superstar. I mostly succeeded too. Except when I was flat on my back with debilitating flu, excruciating back pain, or five-day migraines. I was all on, or I was all off. (Hey, no one does totally sick like a perfectionist. If I'm not 150% sick, I'm not sick … or something.) Trying to be perfect was an impossible goal, because a single flaw, however tiny, is still a flaw. It's a zero-sum game, all or nothing, black or white, yes or no.

So, instead, I decided to be excellent. I know from marking undergraduate essays that a first-class essay is about 80%, and such work is described as 'excellent, scholarly, original'. I loved marking essays that were 80%.

I am delighted to produce excellent, scholarly, original work. So I learned to work to 80%. Sometimes, my work is in a fortnight late. When I submit my work to peer reviewers or writing buddies, I've left some space to integrate their input. Sometimes, I spend the whole budget, sometimes, I ask for a little bit more. I still meet my targets. Sometimes I exceed them, but only if it's easy. I'm not perfect, but I'm still successful, in fact, I'm more successful (I haven't needed a week off for a migraine in years).

Many PhD Students have a mix of low-level perfectionism, imposter phenomenon and perceived procrastination (Lonka et al. 2014; Sverdlik 2020). You are new and on probation in your research field, you need to play close attention to critical details and the timelines are negotiable, so it's never clear how behind you are. So it's not surprising if you fall back on perfectionism as a strategy to deal with it.

But if you don't finish your PhD because you are trying to be perfect, you are not striving for perfection. You are striving for failure. You chose perfectionism over finishing your PhD? You just chose failure. So a better strategy would be to decide to pursue excellence instead of perfection.

You love to be excellent, you love to be exceptional, you love to do brilliantly, you love to succeed, you love to be complete. Perfectionism is stopping you.

We often say 'perfect is the enemy of done'. Voltaire said, 'perfect is the enemy of the good'. I say perfect is the enemy of excellence. Perfect is your enemy.

Instead be excellent, be exceptional, do brilliantly, succeed, be complete.

You just have to choose success. And you are already brilliant at choosing success and pursuing it rigorously, energetically, bravely, persistently. This is playing to your strengths. Research students are already some of the smartest, most competent, most together adults on the planet. This way, your perfectionism problems are pretty much solved, though not totally solved; we aren't doing perfect, we're doing better. So, say, 'Fuck perfectionism, I'm finishing my thesis'.

## Notes

Perfectionism, imposter phenomenon and perceived procrastination have been widely studied in this cohort, including:

Kirsti Lonka, Angela Chow, Jenni Keskinen, Kai Hakkarainen, Niclas Sandström and Kirsi Pyhältö, 'How to Measure PhD Students' Conceptions of Academic Writing–and Are They Related to Well-being?', *Journal of Writing Research*, 5.3, 245–269, 2014.

Anna Sverdlik, Nathan C Hall and Lynn McAlpine, 'PhD Imposter Syndrome: Exploring Antecedents, Consequences, and Implications for Doctoral Well-being', *International Journal of Doctoral Studies*, 15, 737–758, 2020.

The French Enlightenment philosopher Voltaire quoted an Italian proverb to claim that 'perfect is the enemy of the good in the *Dictionnaire
Philosophique: Ou la Raison par Alphabet*. 1770. 'Perfect is the enemy of
done' first appears in publication attributed in conversation to entrepreneur Harris Turner, in Craig Hall, *The Responsible Entrepreneur: How to
Make Money and Make a Difference*. Career Press, 2001. I don't think I'm
the first person to say, 'Perfect is the enemy of excellence', but this seems
to be the first appearance in a book.

A first version of this section was written for *Research Degree Insiders*:
https://researchinsiders.blog/2013/05/01/perfectionism-is-the-least-of-
your-problems/

Some of the material was developed in conversation on:

Kevin Sonney, Host, 'Lucky Little Man', Episode 208. Dr. Katherine Firth,
Productivity Alchemy podcast, 2021, https://productivityalchemy.com/
2021/07/15/episode-208-lucky-little-man-dr-katherine-firth/

## Next Steps

Significant imposter syndrome or perfectionism may require a counsellor or mental health professional to address it.

If you are experiencing exclusion or bullying, or are being told
(explicitly or implicitly) that you don't belong in research, then
explore your university's processes for addressing discrimination and
harassment.

### 7.3.4 Writing towards hope: Can writing be healing?

Writing can be hard. We can feel that writing and rewriting is an academic chore, something that must be done. Or it can feel like a drain, a
strain, a pain. But writing can also be an act of hope, and an act of care
of the self.

A major contributor to the concept of 'self-care' is Michel Foucault, particularly in Volume 3 of his *History of Sexuality* entitled *The Care of the Self*.
For Foucault, the 'care of the self' means the 'cultivation of the self', the
attention to developing and governing your own capacity, whether as a

precursor to stepping out into your community, or in an individualistic society where such care can only come from the self. The cultivation of the self is the purpose of adult education.

This care activity is not soft, or easy. In *Alcibiades 1*, one of the ancient Greek sources Foucault uses to make his argument, Socrates uses a number of terms to discuss the 'care of the self', including to manage or take care of yourself, to make an effort to develop yourself, which Foucault translates as 'cultivation of the self' (ἐπιμεληθεὶς σαυτοῦ, *Alcibiades 1* 120d, 127d, 128d). Thus, the 'care of the self' is the *'epimeleia heautou*, the *'cura sui'*, the making better of the self and your community, for the purposes of living well and being well (*Care*, p. 45).

The care or cultivation of body, mind and spirit is integrated, and it is all necessary. In the practice of reflection and action, writing is an integral part. As Foucault puts it:

> Taking care of oneself is not a rest cure. ... Around the care of the self, there developed an entire activity of speaking and writing in which the work of oneself on oneself and communication with others were linked together. ... Here we touch on one of the most important aspects of this activity devoted to oneself: it constituted, not an exercise in solitude, but a true social practice.
>
> (*Care*, p. 51)

In contrast, self-care as recommended to us by popular culture is frequently about luxury—about buying luxury items and engaging luxury services. And the definition of luxury is something to excess, that is beyond the requirements, it is delightful because it is unneeded. But Audre Lorde, the thinker most foundational for our modern concepts of self-care, writes, 'If what we need to dream ... is discounted as a luxury' then 'we give up the future of our worlds' ('Poetry Is Not a Luxury', p. 28). To consider writing as a luxury is to discount it. The excess cheapens it, makes it worth less, makes it mean less. Instead, we need writing like poetry for our self-care because it is 'a vital necessity of our existence' alongside 'action in the now' to enable survival, pleasure, healing and strength (pp. 26–27).

Similarly, self-care, Lorde writes, is 'necessary':

Caring for myself is not self-indulgence, it is self-preservation, and that is an act of political warfare.

*(Burst of Light*, p. 130)

Self-care is looking after yourself when you have cancer. It's warfare. It's management, command, medical healing, cultivation. It's education, expertise and reflexive practice. Lorde writes of things that are necessary for her to thrive as 'my givens', not negotiable or excessive or something we can discount.

Lorde sees her writing as essential: her lectures, her poetry, her essays and her memoir. She also includes her reflective and developmental practice ('I see and learn', 'ἰδὲ σαυτόν'), and her physical care for herself as a woman experiencing physical and political pain ('I rest', *'cura sui'*), and her situation in relation to community and pleasure ('I love'). Love is not the opposite of writing, we write for our communities, we write for readers. bell hooks similarly described writing as freeing and healing, of writing as 'release', and of the process of writing as a 'place of reconciliation and reclamation' (*Remembered Rapture*, p. 6).

But what about academic writing? Isn't that a different thing? Absolutely not. Particularly if you are doing a PhD, you are literally writing yourself into existence as a scholar. The thesis proves you are an expert, it shows your awareness of your position within the field, it demonstrates that you have grown and developed as a researcher to the level required. Kamler and Thomson have long argued that 'doctoral writing' is 'text work and identity work' (2007, p. 166).

What we should also recognize is that writing and rewriting are not the opposite of self-care. In our drafts, reports, reflective journaling, edits and revisions, we are making an effort to develop ourselves (ἐπιμεληθεὶς σαυτοῦ). We develop expertise and leadership potential, becoming educated, wise, knowledgeable, intelligent, competent at managing projects and teams. This is what we show in a thesis.

For a doctoral scholar, writing is not a luxury, writing is a necessity. Writing is how we get things done in the world, how we make new knowledge, but also how we make space for our new knowledge and share it with our community of scholars. Our discipline can constrain us or care for us. We can develop practices for writing as exhaustion, or as exertion towards our own cultivation. Our writing can be how we experience and re-create the unequal functioning of power, or it can be how we 'taste new possibilities and strengths' ('Poetry Is Not a Luxury', p. 28).

And this is why Lorde argues that 'Poetry Is Not a Luxury':

> As we learn to bear the intimacy of scrutiny and to flourish within it, as we learn to use the products of that scrutiny for power within our living, those fears which rule our lives and form our silences begin to lose their control over us.

(p. 25)

When it is time to face a rewrite, it is a moment to ask if we can use generative or regenerative writing techniques. If our careful revisions can be revisions full of care for ourselves and our community. If in our generous reading of our own texts and our supervisors' feedback, we can offer generosity to ourselves and our future readers. Writing is not a luxury. Writing is not the opposite of self-care. We can write towards hope.

## Notes

Michel Foucault, *History of Sexuality, Care of the Self, Volume 3, Cultivation of the Self*, translated by Robert Hurley. Penguin, 1984/2020.

bell hooks, *Remembered Rapture: The Writer at Work*. Henry Holt, 1999.

Barbara Kamler and Pat Thomson, 'Rethinking Doctoral Writing as Text Work and Identity Work', in Bridget Somekh and Thomas A Schwandt, editors, *Knowledge Production: Research Work in Interesting Times*, pp. 166–179. Routledge, 2007.

Audre Lorde, 'Poetry is not a Luxury', in *Sister Outsider*, pp. 25–42. Penguin 1984/2019.

Audre Lorde, *A Burst of Light: And Other Essays*. Ixia Press, 1988/2017.

Plato (attributed), *Alcibiades 1*, c.390BCE/1927.

## Next Steps

This section revisits thinkers we have previously thought alongside with reference to generous reading strategies (see Section 1.3.5), journaling (see Section 1.3.7) and logical structures (see Section 5.3.2).

## Reflective practice for rewriting: What motivates you?

Now you have read this chapter, it's time to reflect on what you want to take forward and put into practice.

Reflect on the following questions:

- Does rewriting feel like an opportunity to you?
- Are you motivated by succeeding? Does critical feedback feel like it helps you move towards success?
- Are you motivated by working for yourself, or for other people? Who is motivating you right now?
- How will rewriting get you closer to your overall goal of completing a thesis, graduating and changing the world?

You might use reflection tools like journaling, talking to a colleague, or mindfulness activities (discussed in Chapters 1–3 and Section 4.2).

# Conclusion

## 8

# Writing well is not the opposite of being well

The greatest freedom to build a writing life that suits you often happens at exactly the same time that you feel most uncertain or precarious: starting a new research degree, moving to a new research job, or in the gaps between positions. This book doesn't solve the issues of precarity, but it can help you to imagine and put into practice the kind of transition you would like to work towards. I hope this book has encouraged you to reflect on the productivity hacks and strategies that work for you, and to think about creative ways to put them into practice in your writing life.

This journey of writing well and being well for your PhD and the rest of your writing life is one I have had to learn and am still on. I graduated into a global recession and faced challenges along the way, including moving across the world to a city with few contacts, struggling with ongoing health issues, being bullied at work and facing multiple rejections in my writing life (including an earlier version of this book!). I asked other people what they actually did when they wrote, found what gave me joy, was not afraid to experiment, and managed to keep on writing. Slowly, I have learned the strategies that have worked for me to stay as well as possible while writing. Be assured, I did take my own advice, and used the processes and strategies recommended in this book to write it. I benefitted from regularly being reminded to stretch, to connect with my community, to imagine my ideal reader, to be generous in my reading and rewriting.

As Audre Lorde reminded us, self-care is 'necessary' (1986/2020 p. 130) For Lorde, even while battling cancer as a marginalized black lesbian woman in America, writing is not the opposite of self-care, writing is part of her care of the self, part of how she pursued wellbeing in her own body mind and spirit, and how she contributed to the wellbeing of people all over

DOI: 10.4324/9781003307945-9

the world. It is this kind of wellbeing, this kind of writing well, that I hope this book has offered you.

---

**Next Steps**

For more about my journey see Sections I.2.1 and 7.3.2.
    For more on Audre Lorde and necessity, see Section 7.3.4.

---

# 8.1 A mindfulness practice for writing: A loving kindness meditation for your writing

Mindfulness is about being present in the moment with your writing, but there may be difficult feelings there. Maybe your writing has been criticized. Maybe you are aware of a lot of things that need fixing in your draft. Maybe you are writing about material that is difficult or sad. Maybe you are tired or bored. Maybe you are in conflict with a co-author or your supervisor over your writing. That's all pretty common! Sometimes reflecting on a situation just highlights how hard everything is and how tired everyone feels.

It can help to move from rehearsing how badly you feel, to articulating a beneficial wish for everything and everyone around you, including yourself. Mindfulness doesn't necessarily fix anything—the point of mindfulness is mindfulness. So you may find this helps you get into a better headspace for writing or collaborating. But you might not, and that's fine. And wishing others well may lead to warm reciprocation, or not, and that's also fine. This is not a tool like a spell check, this is an emotion and a hope and an aspiration. Researchers are allowed to have those too.

If you'd like to have a go, you might want to start with a traditional global meditation like a *mettā bhāvanā* (cultivation of good will) or apply it more specifically to your writing practice. It might look something like the following words:

Let me be happy and safe now, as I continue to write, may there be joy in my writing.
    Honour to my brain and its way of journeying. May its setting out be blessed with a spirit of safe exploration. Generosity to its methods

of creativity, problem-solving and way-finding. May I honour its journey as much as its destination. You are doing great, brain!

May there be joy and love sent to this computer, which works so hard alongside me. Blessed be its memory, its connections, its processing power, its waking from sleep mode and its recharging. You are doing great, computer!

May there be calm and strength sent to this printer, in its printing, scanning and copying modes, may there be smoothness and clarity in its paper loading and ink application, fidelity in its images. You are doing great, printer!

May there be joy and insight for my co-authors, editors and reviewers. May there be delight in connection and communication. Let there be honesty and generosity in our dealings. You are doing great, writing companions!

Grace and kindness to this chair, this desk, this lamp. May we support one another, holding each other: solid, soft, bright, level. You are doing great, writing furniture!

Love and peace to those around me as I write: to my family, co-workers, or strangers. May your own lives and days be ones of health, happiness and peace. May I bring peace to you, companions who are not writing!

Hello neck, hello back, hello wrists, hello knees, hello eyes, hello jaw, hello temples and forehead. Hello gut and brain and heart. I meet you and send you loving kindness.

Hello notes. Hello plan. Hello analysis and evidence. Hello draft. Grace and mercy to you, kindness to you. May you be happy-minded.

Maybe this sounds like the opposite of your normal thought patterns. Do you think unkind thoughts towards your equipment, writing, and those around you? Do you send them exasperation, frustration or ill will? You wouldn't be alone! There are whole humour genres based on academic snark.

A loving-kindness meditation doesn't mean you should gloss over an injustice, ignore when you are tired or avoid conflicts. But what would it mean if you started from a place of acceptance and kindness for your department printer and your laptop, instead of exasperation or indifference?

Offering kindness to machines, students and employees, helps me turn the dial towards being the kind of human I want to be in the world. Offering kindness to myself and my writing helps me work through my drafts with softness. However harsh the world is to us, we don't need to double it by being harsh on ourselves too. In fact, the less care others offer you, the more important it is to give yourself softness and healing and care.

You may never be the team member who can be found telling the photocopier how much you believe in it (though I am!), but maybe you could dial back on the negative talk, to yourself and others. How does that feel? What grace could be experienced?

---

### Notes

For more traditional *mettā* or *maitr̄i* from different traditions see, for example:
  *Yoga Sutras of Patañjali* (Part 1, *Samādi Pāda*, Verse 33).
  *Chandogya Upanishad* (Part 8, Chapter 15, Verse 1).
  *Tattvartha Sutra* (Chapter 7, Sutra 11).
  *Sutta-nipata* (Part 1, *Uragagga*, Section 8, *Mettasutta*).
  This reflection was also loosely inspired by the Actor Network Theory. See, for example, Bruno Latour, *Aramis, or the Love of Technology*. Harvard University Press, 1993/1996, pp. 225–227 and pp. 778–788.
  A first version of this section was written for *Research Degree Insiders*: https://researchinsiders.blog/2021/09/09/a-loving-kindness-meditation-for-your-writing/

---

## 8.2 A physical wellbeing practice for writing: Celebration dance party

You read this whole book! It's time to have a celebration dance party!

If you want to get pets, kids, office mates or your writing group involved, send out invites and pump up the volume! If this is a party for one, put in your earbuds or close the office door.

Queue up some of your favourite dance music and set the clock for five minutes. It doesn't matter if it's hardcore punk, a classical minuet, a cheesy bop or a dark tango. It just matters that you feel like dancing when you listen to it.

Maybe it's time for those fairy lights or that disco ball. Maybe try it no-lights-no-lycra style and turn the lights off so no one can see you.

Turn on the music and dance!

Tapping your feet and nodding your head counts as dancing, as does twirling, leaping, headbanging or quickstepping. Clap your hands, get out a tambourine, sing along. Get yourself physically involved in the music somehow.

If you are having a great time, feel free to do more than five minutes.

And I am dancing along with you! I am so excited and proud and awe-struck at what an amazing and important writing job you have done!

## 8.3 Moving forward with writing into your future

All my writing books have a version of the writing cycle in them, but this book really focuses on the whole cycle. Writing is not just getting words on a page or spelling them right. Writing is a complex, multi-stage, iterative process, and each stage has different requirements and challenges.

You may already have strategies that help you manage those requirements and challenges. You might be starting in a different place from me: with a different body, family life, brain chemistry, research field, academic background or personality style. That's cool! There is no need for you to follow my practices as the 'right' way to do things. Rather, in this book I reveal how I, and others, honestly work so that you can have permission and encouragement (and maybe a few pointers to explore) to set up a writing practice that you can live with and work with.

This book was proposed as I was finishing a long academic publication for which I needed to do hard, theoretical, painful thinking and research. The topics weren't things you can address lightly, and getting it wrong had the potential to do enormous hurt and damage to others. I really struggled with this content, but I believed it mattered that I did the work. The strategies in this book are about making the process bit of the writing easier so you have brain space and emotional space to deal with the distressing or perplexing challenges of your research.

This book is also about getting better at understanding what kind of hard your writing might be at each stage, so you can plan for it. Hopefully, this book has helped you identify and develop strategies to keep writing into your future: both the next few years of PhD writing, and a long career where writing is an active and fulfilling part of your life.

### 8.3.1 Writing a thesis is hard work, but it needn't be damaging work

Taking the time to be well—to eat food, drink water, have a social life, exercise, lie on the grass and daydream, look up from the screen, breathe deeply, live mindfully, get enough sleep—is not a distraction from your thesis, it forms the bedrock of your writing life. A sustainable, life-giving, self-caring writing life is one that you can keep going beyond your PhD.

As an academic and an author, I need to keep on writing. I need to draft, edit, redraft, rewrite. Getting a book published takes so many stages of edits. The more experienced I get, the easier some things become. But I also find ways to challenge myself, to tackle harder projects. So the writing stays hard.

On my blog, I often talk about writing in relation to making bread, or lifting weights. Not only because they offer useful metaphors for writing, but because they actually are how my writing gets done. My strong hands and wrists from kneading dough and lifting dumbbells allow me to type. The pauses as I step away from the desk help me think, or get critical distance. The calories I consume when I eat the bread, turn into the electricity that powers my brain cells and keep me awake. We are interconnected to our whole bodies.

And we are connected to one another. I believe books that set out punitive, disciplinarian forms of writing advice make writers feel alone and ashamed, and contribute to writer's block and imposter syndrome. Writing books that celebrate all of us, in our all our bodies, with all our brains, help us come together and share. When we have a writing community based on acceptance, generosity and authenticity, then the writing we produce will be ethical, productive, readable and useful—in other words, 'good writing'.

I do not believe that acceptance is the opposite of good writing. Your writing must be original, scholarly and accurate to pass a PhD. Your writing might not yet be great, but together we can make it great. Accepting that you will need feedback, and you will need to rewrite is part of making your writing great.

And as you bring your whole self to the writing desk, you will also start to find your voice as a writer, your flow. You will not just be a competent student of writing, you will write like an expert, like a peer, like an author, like a scholar.

## Notes

A first version of this section was written for *Research Degree Insiders* and republished at: https://www.timeshighereducation.com/blog/should-phd-be-hard

### 8.3.2 Writing well is something we do together

You need a community around you to write well. That community may include your friends, family, housemates, pets, writing groups, writing buddies, and co-authors.

This community might include your supervisors, writing specialists, editors or reviewers. It might include online advice from blogs, podcasts or books. I add some more classics at the end of this section.

Scholarships, annual leave and sick leave, healthcare, wellbeing services, and student services make a major difference to being well and completion rates. To write well, it helps if your institution and the whole of society supports you too. As we make time and space for our health and mental health, we might also want to include professionals in those areas.

PhDs are not only about doing research and writing it down. They are about making a contribution to knowledge, to making people's lives better, either through greater understanding or practical changes to lives and environments. Writing well is therefore also part of doing good. The world can't wait to read the words you write. Let's sit together and get some writing done.

---

### Next Steps

General classic writing resources I'd recommend:
Umberto Eco, *How to Write a Thesis*. MIT Press, 2015.
Elizabeth Gilbert, *Big Magic: Creative Living Beyond Fear*. Bloomsbury, 2015.
Marian Petre and Gordon Rugg. *The Unwritten Rules of PhD Research*. Open University Press, 2004/2020.
Barbara E Lovitts, *Making the Implicit Explicit: Creating Performance Expectations for the Dissertation*. Stylus, 2007.
Rowena Murray, *How to Write a Thesis*. Open University Press, 2002/2017.
Estelle Phillips and Colin Johnson, *How to Get a PhD: A Handbook for Students and Their Supervisors*. McGraw-Hill Education, 1987/2022.
Edward W Said, *On Late Style*. Bloomsbury, 2006.
John M Swales and Christine B Feak. *Academic Writing for Graduate Students: Essential Tasks and Skills*. University of Michigan Press, 1994/2012.

---

## *Reflection practice: Beyond the book*

Now you are at the end of the book, it's time to reflect on what you want to take forward and put into practice.

You might use any of the strategies discussed in the book, or others that you enjoy, as reflection tools.

Reflect on the following questions:

- What will you take forward from this book for the next stages of your PhD?
- What other mindsets, techniques, skills, resources, mentors and advice will you add to your toolkit?

And a second step, if you return to this book as you are ready to move into the next phases of your writing life:

- What served its purpose for the PhD, but will not be carried into the future?
- What helped you during your PhD, and what do you think will help you for the next stages too?

However you write, whatever you take forward, whatever you leave behind, a final *mettā*:

> May you always write with truth and grace, may you write with health and happiness, may you write with strength and purpose, may your writing be supported by communities of co-writers and readers, may your writing help to change the world for the better.

# Index